THE GIFT
& CURSE

One Man's Journey with Dyslexia

DEON L. BUTLER

Published by So It Is Written, LLC
Rochester, MI
SoItIsWritten.net

The Gift & Curse: One Man's Journey with Dyslexia
Copyright © 2025 by Deon L. Butler

Edited by: So It Is Written – www.SoItIsWritten.net

Formatting: Ya Ya Ya Creative – YaYaYaCreative@gmail.com

ISBN: 979-8-9912588-7-6

LCCN: 2025906519

PRINTED AND BOUND IN THE UNITED STATES OF AMERICA

Rich or poor, everyone will face adversity. Gift or no gift, everyone is special. Believers and nonbelievers, there's something higher. Life is a journey. Every step is a gamble. The choices you make in life will determine who you are and where you go. You will make mistakes in life, but the key is to learn from them before it's too late. Use these ingredients in life: love, joy, peace, faith and hope. You're bound to make something special grow. But if you don't believe it, you won't achieve it.

Trust me.

ACKNOWLEDGMENTS

Thank you, God, for loving me first!

To my family: The curse is broken! Thank you for always loving and supporting me.

To Julianna, I'm so blessed to have you in my life. We created something so special. I will always love you!

To my first daughter, Selena Butler: You made this journey all worth it.

To the Makrinos Family: Thank you so much for taking me into your home.

To my late grandma, Adrian Butler: You built a foundation that will last forever. I'm truly grateful.

To my mother, Joycelyn Butler, who's no longer with us on this earth, I miss you so much. I'm thankful for the good and bad days. Thank you for loving me unconditionally.

To my teachers, coaches, mentors, and community: Thank you for guiding me during this journey. I wouldn't be successful without you.

To my tutor, Mrs. Susan Schmidt: Thank you so much for being patient with me. Thank you for teaching me the fundamentals of reading. I no longer feel a storm over my head.

Thank you, Dr. Eric Thomas, for being an amazing mentor, teacher, and coach. As I was searching for answers from God, He led me to you. You are the true definition of hope.

TABLE OF CONTENTS

The Trauma Didn't Break Me

Over my lifetime, I have faced much adversity. One of the biggest hurdles has been my inability to be a proficient reader and writer no matter how hard I tried. Throughout these struggles though, I've never given up. I always wanted to accomplish more. I have been on a journey of self-discovery about my trauma and its impact on my choices. I've also had to face my fears about not being able to read and write as well as my peers. This has affected the entire trajectory of my life personally, emotionally, spiritually, and financially. My plan has been to heal from my past.

I grew up in the 1990s in Inkster, Michigan, which is outside of Detroit. Six boys and two girls all lived in a two-bedroom house. We all had the same mother and father, but I was mostly raised by my grandmother, who I loved dearly. Unfortunately, the trauma I was exposed to has had a big impact on me. I saw so many things during my childhood that I didn't understand. As a kid, I was always so angry, but I didn't know why. I was constantly plagued with so many nightmares. Today, I still have some of the same nightmares. When I was younger, I constantly wet the bed because I was so scared to get up and go to the bathroom.

I didn't stop wetting the bed until I was in middle school. Embarrassing, right?! What I didn't mention was that there were a few people in my family who always came home drunk. There was a lot of fighting. Sometimes, the police had to get involved. Even worse, sometimes someone ended up in the hospital. One night, I remember getting up to go use the bathroom. I got caught in the middle of the crossfire between my family members, fighting like they didn't even know each other. It was the most terrifying thing ever. To watch the hostility and rage that night was shocking.

They threw punches left and right. I watched my sweet, brave grandma stand right in between them. She caught hell trying to break their fights up. After that night of drama, I stopped getting up to go to the bathroom. I'd close my eyes and pretend I was sleeping. That year, my brothers and cousins soon became my enemies because I started peeing in the bed, and they had to deal with my wet spots. All this violence affected my sleep patterns. It was hard to fall asleep, and I frequently woke up in the middle of the night because of the noise. They fought daily, like clockwork.

It was hard watching my grandma deal with that type of pain. She was the type of person who would give you the shirt off her back or her last five dollars. She was a brave soul who stood up for what she believed in. She was a very peaceful woman who didn't take any crap from anybody. My grandma was 5' 2", but she had the heart of a lion. She was very protective of her kids and grandkids, whether they were right or wrong. Alcoholism runs deep in our family, so deep that my grandma had to protect herself from her husband, my grandfather, who was a big drinker. One time when he was drunk, he almost killed her. I never met my grandfather, but I heard terrible stories about him.

He was a war veteran who suffered from post-traumatic stress disorder (PTSD). From what I've been told, my mother and her brothers had it pretty rough. My grandfather beat them for no reason, and he used anything he could get his hands on to hit them with. He used bats, brooms, and even pans. He even burned cigarettes out on their arms as if they were ashtrays. One day when my mother and her brothers came home from school, they saw my grandfather outside, fighting my grandmother.

He was beating her badly. Of course, my mother and the others tried breaking it up, but they were no match for this strong Army vet. That day, my grandfather couldn't control himself. He turned on the kids and beat them. My grandma was half dead on the ground. She could barely see or breathe. However, she was able to turn over long enough to see her kids being abused. That's when her "motherly instinct" took over. She used what little energy she had left in her bones to attack my grandfather with a knife to the stomach. My mother and her brothers watched their father bleed out on the ground. My grandma was rushed to the hospital in critical condition. Luckily, she survived that horrific day.

As you can see, the effects of alcoholism and violence have been a constant thing in my family. My mother's generation continued the cycle. My uncles and aunties drank and violently took their problems out on each other. My siblings, cousins, and I had to deal with the same trauma. Once again, my grandma had to deal with another cycle of alcoholics.

As I got older, I felt like I wanted to protect my grandma. During my teenage years, my heart and love became stronger for her.

On those nights when my family came back home drunk or high, I already had my mind made up to help my grandma. It was my duty. I learned how to take the punches she used to take. Over time, I grew to love the pain. I got hit with frying pans, brooms, bats, and other objects. One day, one of my family members pushed my grandma to the ground during a fight. I jumped over her body and covered her up, using my body to shield her. I looked my grandma right in her eyes while I got kicked in the back and beat with other objects. I didn't understand what I was doing at the time. I didn't think. I just reacted to protect her.

My siblings called me crazy because I was the bravest one when chaos broke out in the house. Strangely, when my family wasn't drinking or fighting, we had the best times. We all stood together, cracking jokes, partying, and building a family bond. To me, it felt unbreakable. We always showed each other love when it mattered the most.

As a kid, it was the most confusing thing to understand.

Little Misunderstood Black Boy

I always knew I was different. I couldn't explain things clearly when I tried to speak like everyone else. My thoughts were never clear. I couldn't pronounce certain words like gas, trash, mask or refrigerator. Older adults loved making fun of me. They made me repeat words often because I mispronounced them. I would say a word wrong, and it would sound like I was cussing. My grandma called it a speech impediment. However, deep down, I thought it was more than that.

When I was in elementary school, I couldn't understand or process the schoolwork the same way as every other student. I used to hold the pencil the wrong way, and I often put my shoes on backwards. I could see the same frustration in my teacher's eyes as I saw in my mother's eyes. I got in trouble a lot in my early school years for behavior issues at school and at home. My grandma or mother used to send me to school with a coat, hat and book bag. When I came home, however, I would only have my book bag, which was usually empty. I have a good memory, but I often got distracted.

Whenever I stepped on school grounds, I got super excited to be with my friends and classmates. I never noticed that I left any of my belongings at school until I got home.

I felt like my mother hated me because she never believed me when I said I forgot it at school or lost it accidentally. No matter what I said, I was still in trouble. First, it started with yelling. Then, it led to horrible whoopings. My grandma was angry with me when I forgot my things, but she tried different methods to help me remember. She would pin my gloves on my coat or have my siblings remind me at the end of the school day to bring my things back home. But these methods only lasted for so long. The last option was to go searching for my things in the lost and found, which I thought was very embarrassing.

In elementary, I was bullied. I also noticed that I couldn't keep up with the other kids with the classwork. I was a really brave kid, and I tried my hardest. However, the teachers, nor my classmates, understood me. I couldn't read or spell my name. I couldn't write in a straight line or pronounce the ABCs. After a while, I started doing other things that made me stand out. I was the first kid in history to skip school in elementary school. I took the principal and police on an adventure.

I had one close friend in elementary school named Dante. Dante was always in trouble and he always got kicked out of school. Dante had a little more experience than I had because he was held back a grade or two. One day, we planned to skip school. I thought it was the perfect idea. During lunch, I was drinking my milk while he was eating his chicken nuggets. That's when we came up with this strategy. I came up with most of the escape plan, while he ironed out the details. I thought it would be a great idea to leave during recess because after recess was nap time. After nap time, we had to read a book. I hated reading time because I had trouble reading. The other students got a star or candy after reading aloud in the reading group. Reading aloud was embarrassing and frustrating. It made me so nervous. I was a little chunky kid who loved candy, but the teacher never gave me any candy, even when I tried my best to read. So, I thought this would be perfect for me to grab some candy on our way out the side door.

My homeboy thought this was the perfect plan. He said he would grab our coats, and we could go to his house after.

He said to me, "My mom is never home."

I said, "Okay. During recess, I'll ask the main teacher to go to the bathroom first, while you ask to go to the bathroom from the teacher's aide. We will meet up in the classroom and leave out the side door tomorrow."

The next day, everything was going smoothly.

I saw that candy and stuck my whole arm in the jar with the biggest grin on my face as I grabbed as much as I could. My boy grabbed our coats, and we went out the side door. We were on our way. It was just that easy. As we walked down the big street, I was super excited. I couldn't stop talking about it. Dante acted like it was nothing. We decided to go to the playground since we'd missed recess. It didn't last long since we got super bored fast. When it's only two kids on the playground, it is not as fun as having the rest of the class with you. So, instead, we went over to his house to play video games. His house was junkier than mine, but I didn't care. We played the game, and I got bored again. I wanted to go home.

He said, "It's not time to go home because school isn't out yet."

"By the time I walk back to my house, school should be out."

In reality, I couldn't even tell time.

I turned to my boy and told him, "I'll see you later."

I started walking home. When I arrived at the house, I tried opening the door. Unfortunately, the door was locked. I saw the neighbor across the street on the porch. I knew him very well. He was the nicest old man.

He called me over and asked, "What are you doing home so early from school?"

Of course, I panicked. I lied. I started breathing hard and went into acting mode and told him the biggest story of my life.

"I got kidnapped. There were two guys in a black car. They grabbed me and threw me into the back seat of their car. I found a way to jump out of the car. That's why I'm home so early."

I didn't think the old man was going to call the police.

"Stay right there," he said. Before I knew it, the whole police force was outside. The police officer kept asking me to repeat my story. I gave him the same story repeatedly with a straight face. I remember it like it was yesterday. The principal came over to my house. He walked in with some of the police officers.

Mr. Woodson was his name. He was a very short and angry man. He kept drilling me about my story. I looked him right in his face and lied as I told him the same story. My grandma and the whole neighborhood believed me. I had great acting skills. Mr. Woodson wasn't having it. He didn't believe anything I said. He took me back to the school and gave me one more chance, to tell the truth. He was yelling and screaming at me, trying to scare me into telling the truth. But I never folded. Needless to say, the cameras told the whole truth. The school staff saw me sticking my whole left hand into the candy jar. I never meant for it to go that far. I was looking for attention. I wanted to feel important like all the other kids. I did get some attention, but it came with consequences.

That day, I received the worst whooping of my life—not only from my family but the whole neighborhood. That's what I mean when I say the community raised me.

The Dumbest, Smartest Kids

Once middle school came around, I believed the rumors others had said about me. People called me stupid and dumb. I was in the fifth grade, and I still couldn't read well. My family already teased me at home about the way I learned. Then, I heard the same jokes at school. My feelings were hurt. The teachers used to call me out in front of the whole class to read, but that only made me more frustrated. People often asked me what I wanted to be in life. I tried telling people my dreams and goals, but it was so hard for me to put a complete sentence together.

My friends used to look at me and say, "Deon, what are you talking about?" In my mind, I knew what I wanted to say, but it just wouldn't come out clearly enough for people to understand. In middle school, I was very energetic and passionate. I never learned how to fully control my emotions. I got into so many fights at home and school. I stuck up for myself, and it often showed in my behavior. My grandma told me all the time, "Sticks and stones may break my bones, but words will never hurt me." That phrase only worked at home with my siblings. So, I started showing people with my fist and anger.

In middle school, I built a different type of image. Since people treated me like I was stupid, I started acting like I was stupid. I got suspended every week. I went from trying to learn in front of the class to making my way to the *back* of the class. Then, I picked on other kids. I didn't pick on the little kids, only the other bullies. As I grew bigger, my peers realized I could fight well. So, I became the bully of the bullies.

I didn't start problems; I just learned to finish them. I was the cool kid who protected the geeks and smaller kids. Deep down, I knew how it felt to be bullied. So, I hung out with a crew who looked different than me. Even though I had anger issues, I always had a great relationship with my teachers. However, not all of my teachers were nice to me. Some of my middle school teachers told me I was no good. They told me I was one of the worst students they'd ever seen. Many people say words shouldn't have an impact on you, but I say it depends on who those words are coming from. The schoolwork didn't come easy to me. I know the teachers got frustrated with me because I couldn't stay focused. But I was a kid with a big heart. I cared for people, and I loved all my teachers.

I often stayed after class and helped the teachers clean up. I tried my best to be nice to my classmates. I'm not saying that I was the best student because I wasn't. I felt like I had to be the class clown to cover up my inability to read. How could I stay focused when the teachers weren't teaching in a way that I could understand?

When parent/teacher conferences came around, I often heard my teachers say to my grandma, "Deon is such a good kid when he wants to be. He is struggling with reading, writing, and spelling, and he can't focus. But he's not a bad kid."

My grandma was so disappointed.

So, for a whole semester, I promised myself I wouldn't get into any more trouble. I really wanted to please my grandma. I gave it my all for a full semester. That meant no fighting, no talking back to the teacher, and no being the class clown. When the next parent/teacher conference came back around, I just knew the teacher was about to give my grandma good news. Unfortunately, the teacher said the same thing from the last parent/teacher conference.

"Deon is a good kid when he wants to be, but his grades are very poor. He's giving little effort in reading and writing."

That next week, I got expelled from Inkster Middle School for fighting. I figured if my grandma was going to receive bad news, it might as well be my fault. I had to move to Detroit with my mother. I truly did not want to move in with my mother for many reasons. We both had the same type of personality: aggressive and short-tempered. Every other night, she came home drunk or high. I knew she would come for me because I never backed down. So, we would fight, and she beat my siblings and me. The next day, it was like nothing ever happened. She couldn't remember anything. My siblings reminded her of the night prior. But I wouldn't talk to her for days because I was the target.

When I was in Detroit Public Schools, I attended Rosa Parks Middle School. I felt like I was becoming a monster. I got jumped by gangs and I was in a fight every other week. I would be at the basketball park when a bunch of teenagers would come over to ask about my shoes. At this time, Nike Air Force Ones were popular. I only had one pair of shoes, and it was the all black Air Force Ones. Everybody wanted a pair. One older boy would tell us, "Run yo' shoes!"

My friends took their shoes off, but I didn't. I refused to give them up. That's when a whole gang stomped me and took my shoes. Your environment truly makes a difference.

Detroit was different back in the 2000s. I got kicked out of the house every other night. Some nights, I slept on the porch because I couldn't control my tongue. My mom would let me back in after I calmed down. I got in so much trouble that I begged my grandma to give me one more chance to stay with her. So, I moved back to Inkster. I was able to get back into the same middle school. I was excited to be back in my hometown.

Here Today;
Gone Tomorrow

I started playing football in eighth grade. I met some good friends on the football team. One of my good friends was Allen Willis. He played quarterback. Allen was one of the best players to play the game. Allen was a superstar around the city. He was such an amazing athlete, but it wasn't his ability to play sports that stood out to me. It was his personality and character. Everyone—and I do mean everyone—loved him.

He was on the honor roll. He also had natural leadership skills. It's true that your friends are a direct reflection of you. I had to pull myself together because Allen had a big influence on me. He told my grandma that he would look after me and keep me out of trouble. I no longer wanted that bully image. I wanted to be a leader. That year, we had a superstar team. Allen could run, jump, sing, and throw. It was nothing he couldn't do. I played tight end. I loved blocking for Allen down the field when he took off running. I had his back.

My boy Orlando played wide receiver. He had hands like glue and was super fast, like a cheetah. Allen would drop back and throw it like sixty yards, and Orlando was right there to catch it.

Then we had Kevin, but everybody called him Pint. He played defense. Kevin could run through a wall. He hit hard. Kevin was the best linebacker in the city at the time. He was one of those players who would make you say to yourself, "I'm happy he's on my team." We were so good, the whole city attended our games. We blew teams out the gate. We could win games just from our defense alone. Kevin was just one of the playmakers. We all had bright futures! The older players and coaches at the high school told us, "You're up next." Everyone was counting on us to be the light of the city of Inkster.

That season, we created a strong bond. We always stuck together. We slept over at Allen's house before the games. At the sleepovers, we promised each other to always take care of one another, like a true brotherhood. That season, we went undefeated. When the football season ended, we had to either play baseball or run track. Orlando and I knew each other the longest because my mother and his mother grew up together, right next door to each other.

Kevin and Allen already knew each other, as well. So Orlando and I played baseball while Allen and Kevin ran track. As we neared eighth-grade graduation, I wasn't really looking to further my education. I didn't feel smart enough because I couldn't read. I barely passed my classes with D's. Orlando and I wanted to make some money in the streets. We posted up on the block and started hustling. Allen and Kevin were track stars. They dominated in every sport they played. Little did we know our lives were about to change forever.

I was with Orlando when I received the worst call of my life. It was the most devastating news. My cousin Mo called me and told me that Allen got hit by a train and he died. My heart dropped. I froze as my phone slipped out of my hand. I looked at Orlando. I couldn't even get the words out of my mouth. I struggled to tell Orlando the bad news. We instantly ran five miles to the scene where everything took place. It was the most terrifying tragedy I've ever experienced in my life. Everything was taped off; people and police were everywhere. Things played in slow motion for me. I couldn't believe it. I *refused* to believe it.

As people gathered around, crying, I saw Allen's mother lose it. Mrs. Willis had a broken heart. She had to watch her son lay on the ground, and she couldn't do anything about it. Mrs. Willis and Allen had a tight relationship. After Allen's funeral, Mrs. Willis wasn't able to recover. She had a mental breakdown. She went into a depression and, years later, died in her sleep.

First, let me explain the area where Allen got hit by the train. In order to get to the high school, you could either go over the train tracks or underneath the train tracks. It was so much quicker to get to the high school if you went over the train tracks.

All the track meets took place at the high school because our middle school did not have a track. That's where Allen and Kevin were headed at that time. They went over the train tracks. Allen dropped his girlfriend's jacket and decided to go back to get it. That's when the impact of the train killed Allen. If you know anything about trains, Amtrak's trains are one of the fastest and quietest in the world. So, it was almost impossible to hear or see the train coming. Kevin saw the entire thing! For a while, Allen's family blamed Kevin for Allen's death. After that day, I never saw Kevin again.

I don't think he ever went back to school. I was at a complete loss. I never believed Allen was gone. One day, I walked down the train tracks to see if he was still alive. Allen was so great in my eyes. There was no way he could just be gone. Our eighth-grade graduation was horrible. The whole school was sick about Allen's death. Just like that, our superstar team had come to an end.

Nobody knows how long we are here on earth. That's why each and every day, we must cherish life. We must love one another and learn to forgive.

Rest in peace, Allen Willis!

The Road to Becoming a Great Leader

Once we got into high school, Orlando went to play basketball. I played quarterback during my freshman year. I took that team undefeated. I couldn't stop thinking about Allen after my final game. For some odd reason, I felt like his death was my fault. When the season was over, I went back home and slammed my room door, crying loudly. That's when my grandma walked into the room. I immediately started yelling at her with so much anger. I screamed with tears coming down my face, "I'm never playing football again!"

My grandma understood my pain. She said, "I don't care what sport you play. What I do know is that you will be attending school if you want to live under this roof."

In my freshman year, I became the man in basketball. I started on junior varsity. I just wanted to forget about everything I had experienced. So, I walked away from football. I finished my freshman basketball season on varsity. I moved up because I performed well. I was super excited about being on varsity. It was every first-year student's dream. I felt so cool being around the older players.

Coach Springer, who was my J.V. coach at the time, told me, "Don't be surprised if you get to play in the games."

I thought to myself, *Me playing in a playoff game on varsity? Yeah, right.* Not only did I get to play in the games, but I hit a buzzer-beater lay-up and scored eight points. We ended up losing in the playoffs. That day, I made up my mind to work hard. I decided to dedicate my time and energy to becoming a better basketball player. My grades were still a problem. I didn't understand how I could work so hard, but I still struggled in school. I tried putting the same type of energy into my school work that I put into sports. However, I didn't understand how to get my brain to work like my classmates.

Yet, somehow, I was able to stay on the basketball team. In high school, I had to maintain a 2.5 GPA. I had to strategize. First, I needed to attend class every single day with perfect attendance. Second, I needed to participate in class. Those participation points added up. Third, I needed to turn in all my school work, which included homework and class projects. It didn't matter if it was right or wrong. Lastly, I had to build a great relationship with my teachers. Apparently, that wasn't so easy to understand because a few of the players on the team got kicked off due to their grades.

The guys who were kicked off the team were some of our best players.

Sports motivated me to go to class. It kept me out of trouble. Being a freshman on varsity meant a lot to me. It was cool playing on the same team as my oldest brother, Lawrence. We both had come a long way in life. Over the years, I watched him become a student of the game. So, it was a dream come true to be able to play on the same team together. After losing that playoff game, my brother, who was a senior, started crying with so much pain. His season ended for good. He was never going to play high school basketball again. He told the young players, "Never take this game for granted because, one day, it will be over."

I took that to heart. I knew he meant every word because he loved the game like no other. That next year, I stepped my game up fully. I already had the experience. My teammates and coaches were counting on me to take on that leadership role. I did just that. I studied the game and learned from the older players. I brought my own swag to the game. I combined hard work with talent. For example, I was diving on the ground, taking charges and rebounding. On the other side of the court, I threw no-look passes and scored a lot of points. I also gave my teammates confidence. I hated losing. I did whatever it took to win.

I was the waterboy, coach, and the team captain. In my sophomore year, we got a little further in the payoffs than we did my first year. Once again, I took to heart what the older players said after the season ended. One of the team captains happened to be my older cousin. He was a superstar in football, basketball, and baseball. His name is Renty Rollins. I learned a lot from Renty—the good, the bad, and the ugly. Renty didn't take shit from nobody. He was a fighter. He was a bully, but he was also a leader. Many people in sports respected him. Renty and I had a lot of similarities, from body frame to family drama. We both were very enthusiastic about sports. So, I watched and learned everything he did. Renty gave his senior speech after his final game, which was similar to my oldest brother's.

Renty said, "Don't take anything for granted because, in a blink of an eye, your high school career is over." Renty didn't cry like my brother, but I knew he meant every word. Renty went off to play football at Jacksonville State. He was a different beast in football. As my junior year of high school approached, my coaches started pressuring me to play football. They called me soft and said I was scared of a little football contact. They also mentioned that I allowed Devin Gardner to take over the school.

Devin was this five-star recruit who came over from the University of Detroit High School. He already had top colleges recruiting him. So, when he came over to Inkster High School, people started saying our school was now Devin Gardner School. People also said he ran me away from football. Nobody knew the true reason I left football but my grandma. I didn't mind them calling me names. But when Devin came over, he just expected me to hand him the crown. Devin and I didn't get along at first. Devin's first year at Inkster High was my junior year. We both were in the same grade. He played quarterback. I have to give him his respect. He was amazing in football. He broke so many records during his first year at Inkster.

Devin was responsible for forty-eight touchdowns that season. Twenty-six of them were passing touchdowns. The other twenty-two came from rushing touchdowns. They also went to the championship that year. Devin Garner's football talent reminded me of Allen Willis. They both were fun to watch and very entertaining. Devin also played basketball at Inkster High. Devin thought he was going to come over and run the show like he did in football.

As you can see, I'm also a superstar. I had basketball on lock! Now, Devin wasn't bad at basketball. He truly is a great athlete. He most definitely was a big help for our team. That year, I won MVP, and we took down some great basketball teams. We had a very dominating basketball team. We went 24-1 during the regular season. Our coaching staff was excellent. They groomed us to be student-athletes who were fully superb. I had a really close relationship with the head basketball coach, Durand Sheppard. He was like a father to me. After practice, he would drop me off and give me long talks on the way home. Coach Shep took care of me. He understood that I wasn't thoroughly disciplined. He also knew that I had a rough life with my family.

I gave Coach Shep a hard time in our first season. No matter what, he always showed me love back. He never gave up on me. Coach Shep knew when my head wasn't in the game. I had a tendency to zone out. He could always tell when I wasn't being myself. Coach Shep would catch me looking into the crowds every few minutes as I checked to see if my dad or mom showed up to the games. He knew that disappointed me. He would call a timeout when we were down by ten or fifteen points. The team huddled around him. He would grab me and shake me. He would yell, "Wake up! They're not coming to the game! We are your family! And we need you here with us now!"

For some reason, that worked. I snapped out of it and made a great comeback. I was the energy booster for my team. It hurt me to know that I was doing all these good things in my life and I didn't have my family's support. My mom did come to some games, but she often showed up high or tipsy. My dad came to a few games, but that's it. What hurt me the most was that I saw players on the team whose families showed up to every game. Their families supported them even when they knew their kids weren't playing in the game.

I never understood why my family didn't take me seriously, especially after all I'd accomplished. My grandma did the best she could, but I knew I needed more support. That year, I felt so much pressure. We won so many games and got a lot of publicity. Not only was I dealing with things at home, but I was dealing with things internally. People often misunderstood me because of my speaking problem. People couldn't understand me. That frustrated me a lot. That year, during the playoffs, I blew my cool! It was one of the worst times of my life.

We were in the middle of playing a team in Jackson, Michigan. If you know anything about Jackson, you know that they can be ignorant toward the Black community. Before the game, our coaches warned us about the referees and the people in the crowd. We needed to watch our temper and not let the other team throw us off our game. One of the players on the other team kept elbowing me in my stomach, and I told the referee. The referee ended up giving me a technical foul! I was confused! I did what I was supposed to do, and I got in trouble for it. I thought maybe it was the way I told him. Before I knew it, my coaches grabbed me. Then, my teammates grabbed me.

I felt like I was in a black tunnel, surrounded by people trying to hurt me. I lost it. Before I knew it, everybody in the crowd grabbed me. The athletic director pulled me into the corner and pinned me against the wall. His name is Greg Carter. Nobody could calm me down but Coach Carter. When he had me against the wall, I looked into his eyes. They were bloodshot red. I saw something different in his eyes. That's when I snapped out of it. Coach Carter didn't even say a word to me. His eyes did all the talking. Because it was halftime, I had to head back into the locker room.

I was embarrassed because I let my team down at the most crucial time. I didn't even get to play in the second half of the game. I had to go sit on the bus and wait until the game was over. When I was on the bus, I wrote a suicide note. I was so ashamed of myself. When the game was over, I gave it to our point guard, J. R. I got off the bus wand walked down the street, feeling sorry for myself. J. R. is a true brother of mine. Once I left, he read my note aloud, and everybody on the bus started laughing and clowning at J. R. for not knowing how to read. It wasn't J. R.'s reading; it was my spelling. J. R. never told them that it wasn't his reading. He covered for me. That day, they won that game by four points. Dan Rice, who was one of the assistant coaches, came looking for me. Once he found me, we walked back to the bus. He told me everything was going to be ok.

That was the game we needed to win to get into The Breslin Center at Michigan State. Then, we were one game away from the state championship. After that game, the team had to meet the next morning to decide what would be my punishment. They had to vote to either kick me off the team, or I had to miss the first half of the game. Of course, Devin's jealous ass voted to kick me off the team. That didn't shock me. Some of the people who I grew up with tried voting me off the team. That hurt my feelings.

My mouth dropped when I saw some of the assistant coaches trying to vote me off. I was almost voted off the team. Coach Shep stepped in and made the final decision. He thought they were crazy for trying to vote me off. He wouldn't allow that to happen. So, my punishment was to miss half of the game in the semi-finals. We played against Flint Powers Catholic High School. They needed me during that game. They were getting embarrassed in the first half of the game. I had to show my support by getting them water and cheering for them. I accepted my punishment. It was harder for me to accept and forgive the people who I loved and knew the longest after they tried to vote me off the team. The coach called my name during the second half to get in the game.

I went right to work. There was nothing Flint Powers could do with me. At one point during the game, I was running back on defense, and I heard the announcer at the table say on live TV, "They could've really used Deon Butler in the first half." I made sure to look out for J. R. during the game. I passed the ball to J. R., and he knocked down huge three-pointers. That was one of J. R.'s best games. I racked up steals, points, and rebounds. I even started guarding their best player and shutting him down.

Before I got in the game, they were down by twenty. After I got in the game, we were only down by four points going into the fourth quarter. We ended up losing that game by seven points. I took the blame for it. When becoming a leader, you first need to become a student. Be ready to accept the things you can't control. Leaders take full ownership of their actions. Leaders also allow others to lead. A leader learns to forgive and move forward. If you are a leader, you must be on the same page with the coaches, your teammates, and anybody else involved with the team. There will be days you may not be in the mood to lead. Those are the most important days of leadership. The coaches are harder on leaders for a reason, so don't take everything to heart. When you master these rules, you know you are a great leader.

Walking Back on the Field

As my junior year ended, I was so hurt that I'd caused my team and my city not to get a championship ring. This would have meant so much for our city. Inkster High was making a big change in sports and academia for all the right reasons. For a while, Inkster was known for a lot of violence. However, when Coach Carter came over to Inkster from Detroit, Inkster became known for athletics. I'm not saying Inkster didn't breed good athletes or win games before Coach Carter came over because they did. What I'm saying is Inkster was never consistent with a winning program.

All the games were packed. Our band was off the chain. Mr. and Mrs. Level, the band directors, made sure our games were packed. If you've ever been to a Black school with an energized band, then you know what it's like. I hated going into the locker room during halftime because I missed the band's great performance. People from all around the country came to the games just to see our band. Our sports teams were outstanding. The girls' basketball team kept winning championships, and our wrestling team was dominating.

Each year, more students went off to college. It was nice seeing students take full advantage of their academic scholarships. In the meantime, I knew I had to take my game to another level if I wanted to be the best basketball player in the district. I showed up to school around 6:30 a.m. to work out. I was lucky because Mr. D. Brown, who was an assistant coach/teacher, lived close to my grandma's house. I caught a ride with him each morning. Mr. Brown was cool. He gave me great advice on how to stay focused and take care of my education. Every day, I worked my butt off in the gym.

Guess who else was in the gym working out at that same time? Devin Garner and Coach Ali. Coach Ali was Devin's quarterback coach. Coach Ali always asked me if I could help out by catching Devin's footballs for him. I would say, "No. I'm working on my basketball game." One morning, I forgot my basketball at home. I was at the gym bright and early. Devin and Coach Ali were in the gym, playing catch. I kept hearing Coach Ali yell at Devin, saying, "Quit throwing the football so damn hard!"

Devin would say, "I'm not! This is just the way I throw."

Once again, Coach Ali called me over to help out by catching the football for Devin. I told him, "No, thank you. I don't want any parts of football."

Coach Ali said, "Deon, didn't I look out for you every time a hall swap came your way?"

Coach Ali was also a security guard. I said, "Yeah,"

Coach Ali asked, "Every time you ask me for money, didn't I always look out for you?"

I said, "Yeah."

I looked at Coach Ali and said. "Yes. I get the point. I'll catch Devin's footballs."

Devin and I started playing catch. I first noticed he was taking it easy on me to see if I could catch the football. Then, he threw the football harder and harder. However, I couldn't tell the difference because I caught everything he threw.

Devin started working on his mechanics by rolling out the pocket and throwing the football toward me. Apparently, when you're rolling out the pocket, that meant the football was supposed to come at me faster and stronger. I still couldn't tell the difference. Coach Ali was astonished. He said, "This boy catches better than Cameron Gordon, and that's saying a lot!" Cameron had just graduated from Inkster High. He was the star wide receiver. Cameron also committed to the University of Michigan on a full-ride scholarship. After a few hours in the gym, Devin asked me if I could start working out with him in the mornings. It felt really good catching the football again. Also, I loved the energy Coach Ali was giving me.

I said, "Yeah. But this doesn't mean I'm on the football team. I'm just catching passes for you and helping Coach Ali out."

Devin said, "Cool. I'll see you at 6:30 a.m."

Every morning, we were in the gym practicing, putting hours of work into our craft. One morning, Coach Carter walked into the gym. He wanted to see what all this hype was about when they told him I could catch really well. When Coach Carter saw me in action, his first words were, "Look at the squirm! He can catch the football, too."

I laughed at him for calling me Squirm.

He called me that because my arms and muscles were small. School had just ended, and it was time for summer workouts and summer basketball leagues. So many people pressured me to play football. I had my mind made up that I *wasn't* playing football anymore. One day, Coach Carter called me into his office to talk about my decision. We talked for a few hours. Overall, Coach Carter said, "Come out to the first day of tryouts. If you don't like it, you can go back to playing softball." He was joking around. He really meant the basketball summer league. I only agreed because Coach Carter was one of my favorite mentors. He treated me like I was his son.

When I went for tryouts, it was something about football that made me feel really good. Maybe it was the agility rush from the high intensity or from the coaches yelling at the players. Whatever it was, I liked it. I tried out for wide receiver. Even though my route running sucked, I still found a way to get open to catch the ball. We had one-on-one drills with the defense backs. I caught everything. No matter where Devin threw the ball, I came down with it. I had a natural talent for catching the football. My decision to commit to the football team came from the last drill of the night, which was defense vs. offense. This had to be the best drill of the night. The defense would walk on the field, talking crazy mess to Devin, especially Dixon. He was this superstar linebacker who was highly ranked in the top players list.

He reminded me of Ray Lewis. He was a straight animal on the field. He would hype up his defense and give them ridiculous energy. All of Devin's key teammates had just graduated. The defense started attacking Devin by saying, "Aww! Poor Devin's all by himself this year." Devin didn't talk too much, but he had a big surprise for them. Right from the start, Devin threw a deep touchdown pass to me. Of course, the defense thought that was luck ... until it happened back-to-back.

Every jump ball Devin threw was a touchdown to me. It was an exciting night. The coaches were hyped. The players on the bench were jumping up and down and running up the sideline. The defense was quiet because they had just found out that Deon Butler was a beast. The 7-on-7 football was the best. None of the players wanted to go home because the intensity was so high. It was something about football that made things supernatural for me. I didn't have to try as hard as I did in basketball. Honestly, I missed football after taking off all those years. I realized after a few practices I could've been a more advanced wide receiver if I hadn't taken three years off.

As I walked into my senior year, I remembered exactly what my older brother, my cousin, and other team captains said.

"Time flies, so take advantage of every opportunity."

I did just that. Our first football game, I didn't hold back. I scored my first touchdown and had seven catches for ninety-five yards. That was just the beginning of my greatness. I couldn't be stopped. I got comfortable by making every moment count. I was blocking, motivating, and making some spectacular catches. We went down to Steubenville, Ohio, and beat the number one team. They hadn't lost a home game in sixty-nine seasons. They had the longest record held in the state of Ohio.

That game was the best. It was like playing in a college stadium. Their fans were the real deal. That game was so packed that their fans were crowded around our endzone. Devin threw me a deep touchdown pass for about sixty yards. I made that catch with my shoulder.

I jumped up and down to celebrate. I noticed their home crowd gave me much respect. It was the best feeling ever. I heard one man saying, "Oh, he's the real deal with that catch." That was one of the toughest environments in which to play a football game. We needed this win to make the playoffs. The game went down to the wire. They scored a touchdown, then we scored a touchdown. This game was back and forth all night until the fourth quarter. Steubenville took the lead in the last few minutes of the game. There were ten seconds left on the clock. The offense huddled up while Devin got the play from Coach Carter. While we were in the huddle, you could feel the low energy we had because we knew the game was over. Devin joined the huddle with faith, though. He had to hype us up.

I already knew what Devin was doing. So, I joined right in with the positive encouragement. We had to motivate the team. We needed to win this game in our minds before we could win the game on the field. Once the play started, things happened so fast. Devin dropped back and threw a Hail Mary to Vorece Sanders. Vorece caught the pass and stepped back while running. He made two defenders run into each other, then he ran into the endzone. We couldn't believe what happened. It was epic. Everybody ran onto the field. It was the best moment in history for us!

Of course, we had good sportsmanship after the game. We shook hands and walked back into the locker room. You would've thought we'd won the Super Bowl from the way we acted in the locker room. We had Coach Carter dancing to rap music. You could tell this game meant so much to the coaching staff because, for once, they took time to have fun after a win.

For the rest of the season, my peers, teammates, and teachers stood in the school hallway holding up one arm as I passed them by on my way to class.

They did that because I made a spectacular one-hand catch. After that game, the team bonded and played a lot better. During the regular season, all of our games were away. We didn't have a single home game. Nobody wanted to play us at home. The season prior, our football team blew the other teams out by thirty points. So, the other teams in the district didn't want to play us. That is why we had to play a lot of Ohio schools or schools outside our conference.

Once we got into the playoffs, teams in our district had to play us.

We wanted to make them feel our pain. We blew teams out of the water. We put up basketball numbers on our opponents. We made it back to the championship. We played at the Detroit Lions stadium. We were up against Lowell High School. After watching them on film, we thought this would be a walk in the park. We couldn't have been more wrong. You should never underestimate your opponent. These big country boys gave us a beatdown. There was nothing we could do to stop them. It felt like the game was over before we even started. Their job was to keep our offense off the field. Lowell's game plan was better than ours. We ended up losing to a good football team.

I knew this was my last game, so I made sure that I had a career day out there on the Lions field. I was unstoppable, with seven catches and 114 yards. I walked off the field with my head up high. As I walked into the locker room, reality hit me. I would never play high school football again. When you put your all into what you love, you truly don't have any regrets. We gathered around as a team. Coach Carter asked the seniors if we had anything to say to the other players. I spoke up with so much love and passion.

"Winning and losing is a part of the sport, but it doesn't define who you are. It's how you respond to the wins and losses that define your character. Football is a family, a brotherhood. Each and every last person on the team plays an important role. Thank you for allowing me to be a part of your family."

I didn't fully realize all the things I had accomplished during the football season because I was genuinely enjoying the moment. After the season, I found out that I made the rank receiver list. This was a surprise to me because I never cared about being ranked or stats. I only cared about winning. In order to find out about the players' stats, you had to look in the newspaper or check the internet. I didn't do much reading, so I never checked to see myself in the papers. But my grandma did. She cut everything out of the newspaper that had my name on it to save it.

That following week, Coach Carter called me into his office. I had a bunch of colleges interested in my ability to play sports. Recruiters in both football and basketball invited me to play at the next level. Coach Carter had so many players going off to college that his office was filled with college recruitment letters. The college letters took over his office. While my teammates were excited about college letters, I was overwhelmed because I wasn't 100 percent sure I even wanted to go to college. During the football season, Devin and I became friends. When I spent the night at his house, he gave me sports gear and a lot of advice on football.

When the season ended, Devin had many colleges recruiting him from all over the country. I got a lot of exposure because I was his number-one receiver. When the college coaches asked Devin to work out, he asked me to work out with him. These were exciting moments for me. These were colleges that I watched on television. One of my best moments was working out in front of University of Florida coaches. At that time, Tim Tebo was a senior, and the Gators needed a future quarterback. I thought Devin would've been the perfect candidate for the job. We had one of the best workouts that day.

The coaches wanted to see Devin's quarterback mechanics, so we put on a phenomenal performance. After the workout was over, the coaches came up to Devin since they were super excited about his skill set. They did everything they could to sell themselves to Devin. One of the recruiting coaches said to him, "We will offer you and your friend a scholarship if you decide to commit to Florida." When I heard that, I thought this would be a great opportunity for us both to take our duo to another level. Plus, this was Florida we were talking about. I know I didn't want to go to college. But Florida would have been an amazing experience.

Devin made up his mind to go to the University of Michigan. I was a little salty, but I truly understood. That day, I went home and lay on the bed, thinking to myself, *I can't believe that I might go to college!* I scared myself because I knew the truth about my education. I knew the truth about how I'd made it to twelfth grade. One day during class, Coach Carter called me into his office. I asked myself, "What did I do this time?" I did my best to stay out of trouble. When I walked into Coach Carter's office, I saw a few coaches standing up. One of the coaches had a Michigan State shirt on. His name was Dan Enos.

At the time, he was the QB coach for MSU. He wanted to get to know me. He was highly interested in me. Dan Enos was from Dearborn, so he loved players from Michigan. He explained his core beliefs and morals: God, family, and education! I loved what he stood for because he sounded like my grandma. I went home and told my grandma that MSU was interested in me. My grandma's smile was so bright that it made me smile. There was one problem: My grandma didn't know my true feelings about college.

I played one year of varsity football in my senior year, and it turned out to be my best year ever in sports. For so long, I held myself back from a sport that I loved to play. The reason I gave up football was the guilt I felt for my friend's death. Allen Willis was my best friend, and he would've never wanted me to stop playing football. I'm thankful for my friends and coaches who talked me back into something that brought me so much joy. I didn't know it yet, but playing football was about to unlock so many great opportunities for me in the future.

The Power of Community

Basketball season was getting ready to start back up. I was still mad at my teammates and coaches for trying to vote me off the team last year. So, I didn't show up to the first two weeks of practice. At first, it started with jokes. A few players on the basketball team started calling me a football player because I didn't show up to basketball practice. The coaches called me, but I stopped answering their calls. I was trying to separate myself from the team. The head coach wasn't going to let me slide that easy.

Coach Shep was smart. It's like he already knew what I was trying to do. Over the past few years of knowing Coach Shep, I learned his routine. After he got off work, he picked up his son from school and dropped him off at home. Then, he headed to our school for practice. I knew his schedule so well that I was able to beat him to the bus before he caught me. I thought I was able to out-think Coach Shep until the day he came up to the school early to catch me before I jumped on the bus. I grabbed all my things from my locker. I was in a rush. I knew every minute counted.

As I ran to my bus, Coach Shep's truck was parked right behind the bus.

He caught me red-handed. Coach Shep called me over to his truck, and we started talking. "Mr. Big time!" he called me. He said that because I avoided him after a great football season. We went back and forth about me playing my last season of basketball. I told him straight up that I didn't want to play basketball anymore. As we were standing face to face, he tapped me and said, "Oh, you're playing your last season." Every player on the team knew that when Coach Shep tapped you a few times, that meant he wasn't playing around. Again, Coach Shep was like a father to me. I only played my last season because of the love I had for him. Of course, none of the players liked my attitude when I got back on the court.

Jerry Jones, who was my high school best friend, improved his game over the summer so much that he ended up getting a scholarship to Duquesne University. It was basically his team now. He also played with my boy Orlando Flicking, who I called my brother. I was okay with them leading the team because they deserved it. However, I wasn't okay with how the assistant coaches and players treated me on and off the court. It's like they forgot who I was and what I did for them. I figured if I treated them like family, they would treat me like family. That wasn't the case.

They wouldn't talk to me in the locker room or joke with me. They wouldn't pass me the ball nor communicate on defense. I felt like an outsider. No matter what, I still found a way to play a great game. I wanted to send them a clear message: They needed me as much as I needed them. We were undefeated at the time. We were about to play a really good team in Detroit. That Detroit team had some scrappy players, and they didn't play around. I decided to miss that game and take my driver's education test. During school hours, I decided to cut my phone off because I knew the coaches were going to call me every chance they got. When it was time to leave for the game, I watched the bus drive off.

Coach Shep usually drove to the game separately, so I didn't have to worry about him at the time. Beforehand, I told Orlando and Jerry my plans. Surprisingly, they didn't even try to stop me. They laughed and told me, "Good luck!" I took my test, and I passed. Since I was already in the city, I went to my mom's house, and I saw my Daddy sitting on the couch watching TV. I gave him $20 to say that I wasn't home because I knew Coach Shep was going to stop over after the game. My dad looked me right in the eyes and said, "I got you, son."

Maybe I didn't give him enough money. Maybe he was trying to teach me a lesson. As soon as Coach Shep stopped over, he ratted me out. I heard my Daddy say, "Deon upstairs." My coach didn't even knock on the door. He walked right into the house. I could tell he was mad from the sounds of his steps walking up the stairs. I acted like I was asleep.

My coach opened my bedroom door and yelled, "I know you're not sleeping! I know you've seen me call you like twenty times!"

I played stupid. I said, "What's going on? What happened?"

"You know you missed the game. We just lost by six points." Coach Shep was furious at me.

We talked for a few hours, and I told him that I was going to pull it together. The next day, the whole team had a big meeting without the coaches. We needed to get back on the right track. Orlando and Jerry pulled me to the side and gave me a summary of how they lost the last game. Orlando didn't hold back; he gave me every detail. I laughed because he told me how tough the other team played. The team they were playing against didn't even let them breathe. After that tough loss, the team knew they needed me like I needed them. Jerry and I needed to get back on the same page if we wanted to head back to The Breslin Center.

I needed Jerry to trust me so I could play my style of basketball. So, at practice, we started going at each other's necks. Every drill Coach Shep called, Jerry and I teamed up and competed. Once the other players saw us going at it like two lions in a cage, they turned up the intensity at practice. I realized I had handed over the crown to Jerry and Orlando too easily. After practice, I spoke up and told them to be ready to battle every single day from here on out. Jerry stood up and said, "Let's get it." We learned that we all needed each other in different ways. That's how I knew we were back on track. We blew teams out. Our season looked like we were headed back to The Final Four again.

At this point in my life, I met with more college coaches. They asked about my grades, and I told them that my GPA was 2.7. That is when I found out that I would need a seventeen on my ACT if I wanted to go to a Division One school. I had already failed the first ACT with a fourteen. So, when the second ACT came around, I needed to be prepared. I asked people if there were any techniques to get a higher ACT score. My friend Shanntay Cheetham and I went to middle school together. She also dated Orlando.

So, we knew each other very well. Shanntay was one of the smartest students in the school. She helped me study and gave me great advice about the ACT. The essay part was extremely important. Shanntay also told me, "If you're running out of time, pick one letter and stick with it." I took a few practice exams, and I passed them. When it was time to take the actual ACT, I took a deep breath and took my time with every question. I took care of the essay first because I knew how important that was going to be. Then, I answered the questions I knew right way. After that, I guessed at the end. After a few weeks, I prayed that I would pass my ACT. I was with my older brother at the time at my mother's house.

I was nervous. After all, this was a big part of my future. My results finally arrived. My family surrounded the computer as we checked my scores. I was too scared to look, so I closed my eyes. The living room was quiet. Then, I heard everybody yelling with excitement. That's how I knew I passed. I received a seventeen on my ACT. My family was so proud of me. My older brother, Lawrence, told me I could get into any college I wanted. This was exciting news for everybody but me.

My senior year flew by. As I walked home from the bus stop one day, I thought, *How can I tell my grandma I don't want to go to college?* Everybody just assumed I wanted to go to college because I got scholarship offers. I assumed everybody who went to college had to be a genius. I had to decide. But I only needed my grandma's approval. I also needed a good reason for not going to college. So, I came up with a plan that caused me to never test my grandma again. When I walked into the house, I had my bookbag around my back. As I headed to my room, I saw my grandma at the corner of the table. She was working on her crossword puzzle. I could tell she was in her zone by the smile on her face.

My plan was to catch her in a good mood so I could jokingly mention that I didn't want to go to college. I thought just maybe she would take it easy on me. I softly said under my breath in a gentle, funny, squeaky voice, "I'm not going to college. I'm going to be in these streets, making money and helping out with these bills."

As I walked to the bedroom, I heard, "What did you say?"

I repeated myself as if I was the man of the house. "I said I'm not going to college."

Before I knew it, she was right behind me, choking me against the wall with her forearm up against my throat. My grandma did this thing where she would wrap her arm under our shirts so she wouldn't get any blood on her hands. My grandma was short, about 5' 2", and very strong. She was beautiful, and she had a loving soul. She had green eyes and long hair. At the time, I was 6' 2" and about 180 pounds. My grandma had me pinned against the wall where the pictures hung. It felt like my feet were dangling off the ground. My head was looking up at the ceiling, but my eyes were looking down at her. I was staring into her eyes, and my heart started pumping fast.

I no longer saw my sweet little grandma. I saw my ancestors who'd sacrificed so much for us. Then, she spoke to me with power and authority. She said, "I didn't work three jobs, took the bus every day to work, struggled to put food on the table, sat in all those parent/teacher conferences, and met with all them teachers for nothing. I took your mother, brothers, and sisters into my house. I used the little money I had to buy you sports gear. I didn't sacrifice so much of my life to hear you say you're not going to college. Best believe that you will be going to college. I don't care what sport you pick."

I felt all the pain in her words. I also felt the pain in my throat. She let me go, and I went right into my room. A few tears fell. I was so frustrated because nobody understood my pain. No one understood that I wasn't able to read well. No one understood how I learned. I wanted to tell my grandma that I couldn't read well. I wanted to tell her I wasn't as smart as my brothers and sisters. But deep down, she already knew. She knew I had a learning disability. However, I don't think she cared too much for excuses. So, that night in my room, I made up my mind that I was going to college. I just had to pick between basketball or football, and I had to decide what college.

I loved basketball with all my heart, but football came naturally. So, I sought advice from my mentors and teachers. I also went to the counselor's office.

I asked Mrs. Norwood a bunch of questions about what it would take for me to graduate. She could see it in my eyes. I was doing everything I could to graduate. So, she didn't mind helping me out and giving me guidance. I was in her office every day, making sure that I had everything I needed to graduate from high school. Mrs. Norwood played a big part in my life. She treated me like I was family. Even after high school, I stayed in touch with her. She later became Dr. Norwood by getting her PhD and becoming a school principal.

I always talked to my mentors about sports. My uncle was one of my biggest fans. His name is Patrick Wimberly. At that time, he worked with the school bus service and the board administration. I could always count on his great advice. I needed help choosing between football and basketball. He broke it down to me, so it made sense.

He said, "The NBA has three rounds in the draft, but the NFL has seven rounds. You basically played one year of football and showed out."

My uncle said, "Think about this when you are picking your colleges and what sport you want to play. You can be a little fish in a big pond, or you can be a big fish in a little pond. Basketball players are 6' 5" and taller, but you have to be a different beast to play football."

My uncle's intellect was so incredible. He later became mayor of the city of Inkster, Michigan. I was thankful to have so many people to count on about my decision. I talked to janitors, teachers, lunch ladies, and security guards about their stories. I took advice from all of them. As my basketball season came to an end, we went deep into the playoffs and lost in the regional finals. It was a bittersweet moment because it was my final basketball game. I'll never forget it.

We had just beaten the number-one team in the state. After that big win, we took every other game as if it were a walk in the park. Then, we lost to a team that was the underdog. They played with energy and passion. Just like that, I walked off the basketball court with all my brothers as we held each other up. For me, it truly hurt saying goodbye, but it made way for me and taught me many lessons. After the season was over, college basketball coaches approached me. Things were starting to heat up. I felt good about my senior year. I won Homecoming King. I became a great leader. Most importantly, I brought my grades up.

It truly takes a community.

College Commitment Day!

I was two weeks away from making the most important decision for my future. Coach Carter was the godfather of sports. He had already sent thousands of players to college. He was my last stop before I made my decision. When we talked, I told him that MSU had verbally offered me a scholarship. I was ready to make my decision. Coach Carter didn't care about what sport I was going to play or what college I was going to attend.

The first thing he told me was, "No matter what decision you make, I'm proud of you for turning your life around."

We talked for a few hours. I felt good leaving his office, knowing that I was going to make the right decision no matter what.

That next day, I received a call from Coach Enos, the assistant head coach at MSU. He said, "I have just taken the head football coaching position at CMU." He made it very clear that it was up to me if I wanted to continue my scholarship offer with MSU. He also offered me a scholarship to CMU. My grandma and I really liked Coach Enos! We loved everything he stood for. I'd heard of CMU, but I didn't know much about it. Michigan State is a big-name school with so many opportunities.

It wasn't too far from home, and my favorite color is green. Then, I remembered what my uncle said.

"You can be a big fish in a small pond, or you can be a small fish in a big pond."

That's when I decided to follow Dan Enos and play football at CMU. Most players go for the big-name schools because of the school's reputation. They also think the name of the school gives them a higher chance of going to the NFL. I looked at it differently. I didn't care what school I was going to attend. I needed somebody who was going to help me grow in all areas of life. I did some research on Coach Enos and his coaching staff. They put God first, then school. Football was last.

I was in a complicated dilemma because the CMU basketball coach also offered me a scholarship. I built a strong relationship with the head basketball coach, Trey Ziegler. His son, Trey Ziegler, Jr., had just won Mr. Basketball in high school. Winning that trophy meant you were the real deal in basketball. Whoever won Mr. Basketball was up against every basketball player in Michigan. Trey Ziegler, Jr. committed to CMU that same year as I did. Mr. Ziegler did everything in his power to get me there for basketball. I strung him on like I was ready to commit to basketball so I could keep all my options open.

I had to call Mr. Ziegler on the phone to let him know that I was attending CMU but for football. When we talked, he sounded highly disappointed. He said, "Good luck!" and hung up the phone. I laughed because I knew that it wasn't personal. It was only business. After making my decision to commit to Central Michigan University, I told my grandma first. She didn't have any words. The way she looked at me said everything. Emotionally, she was so strong. I could tell that she was extremely proud of me. She fought back tears. She wanted to cry, but she had to be strong. My grandma was a woman raising a young Black man. She did everything to teach me how to be strong.

When I gave her a hug, she was fighting even harder not to cry. Finally, I understood why she was so hard on me all those years. She was my mother, father, and grandma all in one. She witnessed so many of our family members go to prison, fall short to drugs, and even die. The bad times broke her heart. But to see me go off to college gave her much joy. On signing day, the athletes who were going off to college had to make a public announcement in front of the whole school and city.

I told the world that I'd chosen football and that I'd be attending Central Michigan University in the fall. The support of the city of Inkster was amazing. Many people were surprised that I picked football over basketball. But no matter what, the community supported my decision. A few other players, classmates, and friends were also attending CMU in the fall. I didn't feel so alone when I found out Crystal Bradford, Jonthen Taylor, and Lamar Walker were all attending CMU. Since prom was coming up, I hit up my big cousin, Willy, and he looked out for me.

He gave me some money and told me to continue being great. I also hit up my big cousin Mo, and he got me fresh. My godfather, Eric Pate, helped me rent that new 300C. I felt like the man of the year. I also looked like him too. I enjoyed prom. The fellas and I got together one last time before the day was over. We chanted in a circle, screaming, "Oh, boy!" We did this before every game and we wanted to chant it one last time. Next was graduation. We had one of the largest classes of 2010. After I got my high school diploma, I walked right over to my family members and gave them hugs and kisses.

I never thought I would graduate. It was one of the best feelings in my life. I'd just achieved the unthinkable. I got my high school diploma by only reading at a fourth-grade level. I went from getting kicked out of school every other day to being a superstar in sports. I went from the teachers telling me that I was one of the worst students in their classes to being one of their favorite students. I ended my high school career with a bang! I gave it my all, and I was rewarded for my good deeds and effort.

I'm grateful for the people in my life who helped me stay on track. I'm grateful for the ones who believed in me most. But this was only the beginning. My life was about to change forever.

A Fresh Start

Even though my grandma was so excited about me going to college, I was worried about her. I knew my grandma could take care of herself, but it was hard for me to leave her side. It was even harder to leave her in a house that was full of violence. I knew once I moved out, things were only going to get worse. I was my grandma's bodyguard. My grandma wanted me to spend the next few months with my mother before I went off to college. So, that summer, I lived in Detroit. When my mother was sober, she was the best person to be around. She cooked, cleaned, and joked around often. I loved that side of my mother.

My big brother Lawrence couldn't wait for me to go off to college. He was just as excited as I was because we both dreamed of this moment since we were kids. He helped me out during my workouts so I could be prepared for summer camp. The coaches sent all the new incoming freshmen a workout manual before we arrived. Lawrence and I went up to the University of Detroit and trained every day until it was time for me to depart. I wanted my grandma to drive me up to school, but she said it would be best for my parents to take me. My grandma wanted my parents to be a big part of this change.

My hometown community put together a care package for me. My church gave me a few dollars as I was about to be on my way to start a whole new journey. It was hard saying goodbye to the environment I'd grown up in all my life.

As I packed, I started doubting myself again. I was scared that people were going to find out about my education level. But it was too late for me to turn back. As I was leaving, I hugged my sister and brothers. We joined together for a big family hug, and then they watched me drive off to college. Mount Pleasant was only two hours from Detroit, but it felt like four.

When I arrived on campus, everything became a reality. Mount Pleasant was a nice-looking town. It was clean and structured. It was the beginning of the summer, and the weather was nice. We parked and unpacked my things. I was a bit embarrassed because I didn't have that much to unpack. I went to college with just a gray container and a book bag. As I was unpacking, I looked around. I saw the other players on the team bring in all these nice things. They had big-screen TVs, dressers, bikes, and other cool stuff. They were loud and excited about college. Once we got up to my room, my mother tried to cheer me up because she could sense that I was down and sad.

Even though my mother and I had our issues in the past, we still found a way to understand each other. It was a great call for my grandma to have my parents with me. My mother knew exactly what to do once we got to my room. She unpacked my things, made my bed, and organized my stuff. It was the best feeling for me. I could see the joy and happiness in my mother's eyes. My dad and I took a walk around the campus. I saw how excited he was for me. He wasn't big on showing his emotions, but I could feel the love and happiness.

We walked over to the football stadium, and the field was huge. He couldn't wait to attend some football games. I pictured myself making big plays and living my dream as a football star. Once we got back to the room, I saw the work my mother had done for me. My room was amazing. She made me feel like I was home. She had my shoes lined up, and she folded my clothes. My toothbrush and toothpaste were in the bathroom. Afterward, we all went down to the cafeteria as a family. We talked and had lunch. This was a different feeling for me. I don't know how to explain it, but I felt like I had the perfect mother and father. We had a great time laughing and joking around.

When it was almost that time to say our goodbyes, I didn't want them to go. I also didn't want to be on my own. As I walked them to the car, my mother wanted to hold hands. So, she grabbed my hand and held on tight. She started crying, and she told me how much she loved me. It was hard not to cry. I had such a wonderful time with them that I didn't want to say goodbye. I even witnessed my father having an enjoyable time. My emotions were all over the place. Part of me wanted to cry, but part of me wanted them to feel the pain and trauma they put me through. Overall, I was so thankful! That day, I felt like I had a mother and father who genuinely cared about me.

My mother gave me the longest, most comforting hug ever. My dad looked me in the eyes and said, "I'm proud of you, and we will be back to visit you soon." Just like that, I was on my own! I was walking into another chapter. I stayed to myself that whole summer. I wasn't really open with my peers. I had one or two friends. But for the most part, I wanted to be alone. I looked at college like I had just walked into prison. I wanted people to know that I was here to do my time. It was nothing personal, just business. A few of my teammates noticed that I wasn't eating lunch with them or hanging with them after practice.

They did their best to open up to me, but I already had friends at home. It was pointless making new friends.

Truthfully, I didn't want anybody to judge me. I was poor. I had a poor education. And I had a bad attitude. It was bad enough that I didn't feel like I belonged. But to be around a bunch of rich, smart, snobby kids was the last thing I needed. Summer classes were about to start. The coaches and guidance counselors helped us get familiar with the campus. They walked with us to our classes. They made sure we didn't get lost and that we made it to the study table on time. I felt really good about summer classes. I enjoyed getting the extra help because I needed it. Summer classes felt like a piece of cake. I did really well. I got my first 3.0 ever in life. I was so excited.

That boosted my confidence in a way I really needed. I called my grandma and told her the good news. She was so proud of me that she started laughing and cracking jokes. My grandma's sense of humor cheered me up because she was very sarcastic, and I understood her. The summer football camp was a different beast. The first two weeks were easy on us. We weren't overwhelmed. That third week is when I started feeling the pain from the conditioning. Coach Perry was our strength and conditioning coach.

He was one of my favorite coaches. He most definitely allowed me to be myself over the years at CMU. That third week of conditioning, when the whole freshman class wanted to give up, Coach Perry said, "Who is going to be the leader in this group and stand out?" That's when I took my shirt off and started screaming with five-pound dumbbells in my hand, saying, "I'm going to be the leader!" Everybody laughed, even Coach Perry. I was this skinny kid with a bird chest, acting like I was already the man of the weight room. I stood out that day. I always felt like I needed to do something at the moment, even if that meant making people laugh to distract ourselves from the pain.

It worked. In the locker room, my teammates laughed about it. As the fall semester started, I felt really good about how the summer ended. College seemed to be a lot easier than high school. Boy, was I about to have a rude awakening! More students came back to CMU after their break. I needed to talk with my school counselor, Ms. Tera, before picking classes. I told her I wanted to go into sports management.

I figured since I played sports, picking this major would help me hide my reading and spelling problems. Ms. Tera explained what classes I needed to take to go down that path. One of the classes I needed to take was Intro to Sports Management. Since I knew a lot about sports, I figured it would be an easy class. I never felt so embarrassed in my life. The teacher asked the class a question about a *city*, and I raised my hand and named a *state*. The entire class laughed at me. The teacher also laughed.

The professor said, "You're not going to make it in this class. I don't even know how you made it to college."

I didn't know my states from my cities. I was used to my peers laughing at me. I knew I could be the class clown. But when the teacher laughed at me, my feelings were truly hurt. That's when I blew a fuse! I had to sit through the rest of the class, feeling like I didn't belong. I felt like the professor should always help students, especially at the college level. After class was over, I walked back to my dorm room. I was pissed off.

I called my grandma to explain what happened. Of course, I didn't make any sense. I couldn't talk clearly. I was yelling and screaming at her, trying to get my point across. She said, "Boy, who are you yelling at?"

I said, "Granny, you're not listening!"

Again, I tried to explain. She said, "Again, who are you talking to in that tone of voice?!" But this time, her voice got louder and more direct. I calmed down enough to use my inside voice.

I knew I didn't belong there. The teacher basically called me dumb. Everybody laughed at me because I gave what I thought was the right answer.

My grandma said, "Okay. Now we are getting somewhere."

I struggled in a few classes that semester. My grandma gave me some great advice. What she said to me that day changed my life. She told me, "There is nothing wrong with asking for help."

I was looking for a way to come home just to prove my point: I wasn't smart enough for college. But I always listen to my grandma. I knew she wouldn't steer me in the wrong direction. The next day, I walked right into the disability office with my head high and my shoulders back, and I asked for help.

About seven or eight people were working in the office that day. They all stopped and stared at me. I didn't know why everybody was in shock until the main director, Mrs. Susie, called me back to her office. Mrs. Susie later became my disability officer. She explained to me why everybody was staring at me. They'd never had anybody walk into the office so proudly as I did.

She said, "You are this 6' 4" tall football player, African American male, who wasn't scared to ask for help. We've never seen that before. Normally, people come to the office shy or because someone forced them to be here."

Mrs. Susie was honored to collaborate with me.

After my grandma faxed over my high school history paperwork, we came up with a schedule and started our work together. The learning disability office came with so many benefits. I got more time on my exams. I could take my tests alone, with no distractions. Because I struggled with reading, Mrs. Susie read to me. Something amazing happened when she read to me. I was able to figure out the right answers by just listening. At that point, I realized I wasn't dumb or stupid. I simply struggled with reading. After a few months of working with the learning disability office, my grades were back on track. So was my confidence.

I dropped my Sports Management class and took a different career path. I thought about being a massage therapist since I was good with my hands. When you can't read or spell, college can feel like a nightmare. I learned that when you face your weakness, it becomes a strength. I was looking for any reason to prove to myself that I wasn't smart enough for college. However, what I found out was that I just needed a little extra help. Instead of hating my professor, I needed to thank him for giving me the motivation and fuel to prove him wrong. If it wasn't for him, I would've never discovered my fullest potential.

"When times get hard and you want to give up, stop for a minute to take a deep breath. I want you to know that everything will be okay."

A Taste of Freedom

The freshmen football players must have had enough of my ways because they started pulling pranks on me. Every day, they pulled a new prank. They did the craziest things to get me out of my room. At first, it didn't work. But they were so persistent and annoying. I tried my best not to feed into their schemes, but my anger got the best of me. They did petty things to trigger me, like cutting the game off while I was playing NCAA football for money. If I was on a date with a little honey, my teammates kept interrupting by asking for something they knew I didn't have. They also cut the lights off while I was in the shower or on the toilet.

It was the last prank that made me lose my cool. It took me over the edge, and I was ready for war. It was a well-planned prank, with at least five football players involved. They filled up a trashcan full of water and tilted it toward my door. The players knocked on my door and then ran down the hallway. I opened my door, and water spilled everywhere. I saw them run down the hall and split up.

Three of them went to the left, and two of them went to the right.

I wasn't the fastest on my team. I had to chase some of the best athletes who were the top players in their high schools. I ran with anger and frustration, so I was bound to catch one of them. I knew I couldn't catch the guys who went to the left. One of the players was a strong safety on defense. Avery Cunningham was the fastest freshman on the team. Eventually, he went to the NFL. The other players were fast, like jackrabbits. I saw Mike Kinville, who ran to the right. He was a linebacker. I knew I could catch him. When I caught him, I tackled him. I had my fist balled up, ready to throw a blow. But he turned around laughing and said, "We're just joking with you. All we wanted was to be your friend."

I laughed and played it off.

I said, "Oh, y'all just joking? I'm joking, too." After that day, I hung out with my teammates and made new friends. Our relationships grew into a brotherhood. I started to like college more, especially when I heard about the refund checks. That's the money you receive from the government when you are in college. I took advantage of every opportunity that came my way to help my grandma out. When I received my refund checks, I sent them back home to my grandma. I knew she needed the money more than I did.

My mother and siblings had to move back in with my grandma because they got evicted from their house in Detroit. That put a lot of pressure on my granny. So, sending my grandma my refund checks didn't bother me. We had a really nice cafeteria. The athletes got unlimited swipes to get into the cafeteria, so that made my life a lot easier. Don't get me wrong. I wanted to enjoy my money like every other college student. However, I had to figure out what was most important to me. Seventy percent of college students waste their refund checks due to a lack of financial wisdom and money management skills. The other 30 percent of college students either saved their refund money because they were already ahead in life financially or they were trying to get ahead in life financially.

I learned that all college students are not just rich, bright, and snobby. Some of them had the same problems I had, if not worse. My teammates saw something special in me, but they also saw that I was struggling with other life issues. I'm thankful that they didn't give up on me; they helped me get through some of my worst times in college. I also learned that I'm allowed to have fun. I noticed when things were going wrong back home, I attached myself to their problems. I had the most fun in college when I wasn't worried about the things I couldn't control.

God Has a Plan

As school got better, football got harder. The coaches loved my work ethic. They applauded my ability to catch the football. My talent on the football field was developing quickly. But the playbook slowed me down. I often ran the wrong plays. I knew what the problem was, but I was too embarrassed to let any of the coaches know. When you constantly screw up the plays, you can't blame anybody but yourself. I couldn't get anything right.

For the first few mistakes, the coaches and team captains blamed me for just being a rookie. After a while, the team stopped giving me excuses. The whole offense had to run suicides after my mistakes. (Suicides are when players have to run the whole football field without stopping.) The coaches soon learned that running suicides didn't help me learn the playbook any sooner. The coaches thought of different ways to help me. I studied the playbook after practice for an hour most days. I even missed a few practice sessions to study the playbook.

I tried my best, but I couldn't read the instructions. I couldn't understand the concepts. It was so frustrating that I thought about quitting. It wasn't just frustrating for me; it was also for the people who were trying to help me. I collaborated with quarterbacks, wide receivers, and graduate assistants. But once again, I felt like a failure. In my mind, I was a failure. That's when I started getting into trouble in the football meeting rooms. I became a distraction to my teammates. I cracked jokes. I got up every five minutes for water or food. I often caused a scene. The coaches kicked me out of many meetings. In my first season, I received my red shirt. That meant I had to sit out for the games my freshman year. I also got an extra year of football.

I was upset at first. But deep down, I knew I wasn't ready. I needed more time to develop my game. As Christmas break approached, I was excited to go back home. I missed my family and friends. I didn't know that things wouldn't be the same after being away from home only a few months. My friends at home seemed different. Home didn't feel like home.

Well that Christmas break was the last time I was allowed to go back home. One day on Christmas break, I decided to visit my old girlfriend. She was hanging out at her grandma's house. She wanted me to drive her home. She also asked me if I could drop her little brother off. I agreed. They started arguing in the car. I didn't know why, but I figured it was a family thing. I reached back to shake her brother's hand, but he smacked my hand away. Then, he threatened me. I was so confused. I thought I was doing the right thing. He said, "Let's fight. I can beat you down."

His sister kept telling me to ignore him. When I arrived at their house, he got out of the car. He beat on my side of the door and screamed, "Get out and let's fight!"

I got out and asked him, "What did I do?"

He kept saying, "I don't care if you're bigger or in college. I can still knock you out." So, he charged after me. I had no other choice but to protect myself. I dropped him with a one-hitter quitter. I asked him to stop, but things only got worse. He charged after me again. So, I hit him again. But this time, I saw something fly out of his hand. It was a knife. He got up off the ground and ran. As I walked to the car, I felt dizzy. Then, his sister screamed. I looked down at my arm, which had blood squirting out of it like a water faucet.

As I tried to make it to the car, I collapsed. My older sister's friend just happened to drive by and she saw me on the ground. They picked me up and drove me to the hospital. It was a blessing because the doctor said I just made it in time. He stabbed me in the artery, and I almost died. When I woke up in the hospital, my family and friends were there for support. Of course, I had a few people ready to ride for me and go to war. But it was my older brother who kept me level-headed. That day, I made the right decision. Even though I was angry, I didn't want anybody else to get hurt. I had to forgive him and find peace within myself.

When I got back to school, I had to miss the whole winter season due to my injuries. The coaching staff thought it would be best if I stayed at school during breaks. I couldn't understand at the time. It felt like I was being punished. I was at the wrong place at the wrong time. I don't think they believed me. After that day, I wasn't allowed to go back home. I only went on certain occasions like holidays or funerals. When I did go home, I had to check in with the coaches every hour by text or call. I spent most of my time at CMU. That's when I started volunteering more around campus.

Sometimes, when we are in the middle of transforming, we can't see it or accept it. We have to trust God and His support system. Everybody started noticing my talent around the city. I started shining. I visited elementary and middle schools in the community. It was some of my best times. I danced and joked with the kids as they enjoyed my entertainment. Before I knew it, I had more requests to show up at events. Instead of reading to the kids, I told a lot of football stories. I also emphasized how important it was to take care of their education. What I enjoyed the most about visiting the younger kids was that I got to play games with them, like Sharks and Minnows.

I was the shark that tried to catch the kids who were the minnows. They would run around the gym, screaming and having fun. I felt like I'd finally cracked my shell. I felt like I'd found my calling. I enjoyed working with youth. It amazed me that I went through all that pain and suffering yet still found a way to naturally help others smile. I made people happy by just being my authentic self. I called my grandma with more good news each week. She could tell I was growing up and adapting to my new environment. Everything happens for a reason.

God knew I needed an upgrade in my life, but I was too stuck in my old ways. I was holding on to so much that kept me from my highest self. Thank You, God, for never giving up on me!

The Love of My Life

As the school year neared the end, I got out of class one day and walked to the cafeteria. That's when I saw the love of my life. This girl was short, with long hair and green eyes. I felt like I was in a movie. Everything moved in slow motion. I watched her as she walked past me with her teammates. She looked like she was from a foreign country. At that time, I didn't know about different ethnicities. I only knew Black people and White people. I said to myself, "I have to get her number."

I walked right up to her and said, "I'm going to marry you one day!" She laughed. She must have thought I was joking or maybe even crazy. I asked for her number, but she turned me down. It didn't hurt my feelings. She didn't know it yet, but I was going to make her my girlfriend. I asked for her name, and she said, "Julianna." When I asked her if she had a nickname, she said, "Jules." I could pronounce Jules. Getting her name was a great start. I saw her studying often. I didn't know what sport she played, but I loved how smart and dedicated she was to her schoolwork.

For the longest time, I looked at study table as a punishment. But knowing Jules would be there made me want to show up every day on time. All freshmen and sophomores needed to complete twenty hours a week of study table. So, I did everything I could to find out her studying hours. Even after I had finished all my work, I stayed just to see her. I found out she played field hockey. I knew nothing about that sport, but I was determined to find out. I found her Facebook profile and added her as a friend. I also knew one of her teammates, Skylar. Skylar and I were huge Green Bay Packers fans.

I found out Jules was from Pittsburgh, and she was a big Steelers fan. When we passed each other in the hallway, we joked about whose team was better.

After a few jokes and what I thought were flirty moments, I thought Jules was definitely interested in me. Nope. I was wrong! Jules turned me down a few more times after I asked for her number. She told me, "I just want to focus on my schoolwork." That's when I started taking my schoolwork a little more seriously, hoping she would notice me. I prayed for any opportunity I could get with her. The Green Bay Packers made it to the Super Bowl that year. They were playing against the Pittsburgh Steelers.

I wrote Jules on Facebook and asked if she would watch the game with me. When she agreed, I was super excited. I jumped up and down on the bed and told myself that I was the man. I also thanked God because He'd clearly heard my prayers. I had to calm myself down. I had to tell myself it wasn't a date. I did everything in my power not to blow this opportunity. I hit up my teammates Jerry Harris from Florida and Jaleel Addae, who later got picked up by the San Diego Chargers. They were hosting the Super Bowl party at their house. That's where Jules and I watched the game.

Jerry and Jaleel were big Steelers fans, as well. Our former college teammate, Antonio Brown, who was drafted by the Steelers, had a big game during the Super Bowl. Of course, Jerry and Jaleel talked a lot of trash. I was the only diehard Green Bay Packers fan who was surrounded by Steelers fans. I held my own. I kept my cool. I didn't push myself on Jules to like me. I was myself: silly and energetic. My boys, Aaron Rodgers and Jordy Nelson held it down. This was probably one of the greatest Super Bowl games ever. It was a close game, but Green Bay won. The final score was Steelers 25 to the Packers 31. This was a great night for me.

After the game, I walked Jules back to her dorm room and told her that I had an amazing time. Jules felt the same way. She thanked me for having a good night, even though the Steelers lost. Later that day, Jules sent me her cell phone number on Facebook. Once again, I was jumping on my bed, acting like a little kid on Christmas morning.

I texted Jules and asked, "Would you like to hang out at a party with me?"

She said, "Yes."

We slow danced and held hands. My boys said I was in love. Afterward, I took Jules to McDonald's. I bought her a McFlurry and walked her back to her dorm room. I knew I wasn't getting a kiss; it took me almost three months to get her number. I gave her a hug, and that's when I saw her smile. I said, "Good night," and walked back to my dorm room.

I called my grandma and told her I was in love. She jokingly responded, "Boy, please!"

I told my grandma all about my night. Jules and I talked on the phone every day and every night. When school ended, the coaches allowed me to go home for a day or two. While we were out of school, Jules and I grew closer. One day over break, Jules' best friend Danielle jumped on the phone. They both were acting strange. I could tell something was going on, but I didn't know what.

Danielle asked me a bunch of questions. They acted like little girls who were in high school. That's when Jules took the phone and asked me out. I smiled, and of course, I said, "Yes!" I knew it was just a matter of time. My grandma and my mother loved Jules and how well-mannered she was to her elders. My grandma also admired how seriously Jules took school. Facetime wasn't around yet, but we did have Skype. That's how we were able to see each other.

My grandma's first words to Jules were, "You must be the reason why Deon is keeping his grades up." Everybody in the house laughed. It was nice seeing my grandma and Jules get along well, especially when Jules traveled from Pittsburgh to visit me in Michigan.

I was attracted to Jules for many reasons. First, I saw the same features in her that I saw in my grandma. I needed to be with someone who put God first. I needed someone intelligent and respectful. It had to be someone who wasn't going to judge me about my past or my education level. I needed someone who was going to help me, not hurt me. Jules was the perfect girl for me. I know college isn't for everybody. But college opened up a new pathway of opportunities and hope for me.

At first, I hated the thought of college. Eventually, I didn't even want to go back home. I'm thankful that I listened and followed my grandma's rules: God, family, and education.

How the Special Olympics Changed My Life

Because I stayed on campus during the summer, I needed a job. Normally, the athletes who stayed on campus for the summer worked for the moving crew. The moving crew's job duties were to clean the dorm rooms, move furniture, and take out trash. Even though I loved working with my hands and doing hard labor, I was persuaded to apply for the Camps and Conferences job. Camps and Conferences hosted a lot of youth camps and events. A lot of people applied for the Camps and Conferences job, but only the best were selected. The pay was great, and it came with a lot of benefits.

I had already built a good reputation on campus by working with kids and being outgoing. This was another great opportunity for me to get more experience. Thanks to the hall director and soon-to-be residence manager, Ms. Steely, I got the job. Everybody loved Ms. Steely. She treated everyone fairly, and she did her best to make sure everyone felt important.

In my first year collaborating with Camps and Conferences, I made the best impression. I did so well that my coaches heard about it. A few of the coaches called me a superstar during football meetings. I became that person who was recommended for every big event or sports camp. One day, Ms. Steely called me into her office. We talked about how much of an impact I had on the organization. She highly recommended that I volunteer for the Special Olympics. Truthfully, I didn't know what to expect from The Special Olympics. I didn't have any experience working with disabilities. I heard a lot about this event. They hosted thousands of athletes and it was a big deal. One of the main reasons I didn't want to be involved was because of my limited vocabulary. I didn't want to be that person who used the wrong words in the wrong way. In my opinion, words hurt. Ms. Steely also mentioned that I could get three credit hours toward my GPA.

There's no way I could turn down three credits, especially if I didn't have to do any schoolwork. So, I decided to volunteer. This was one of the best decisions I made in college. When I volunteered, my eyes were opened to a whole new experience. It was basically a three-day sports Olympics for athletes with various disabilities. Afterward, everybody came together to party.

I met some of the most amazing people in the world during the Special Olympics. The excitement and fun the athletes had during their sports event made me want to forget about all my problems.

These athletes didn't care who was watching. They had a good time, no matter what. I felt the same way. I danced, sang, motivated, and signed autographs. I can't even put into words what the Special Olympics did for me. I was able to be my true self without anyone judging me. I didn't have to put this tough person persona on. I could be happy. The athletes welcomed me with open arms. It's like they felt the pain and struggles that I'd dealt with for the past few years. I gave out hugs, high-fives and positive vibes. It didn't matter if I couldn't read, write or talk straight. They accepted me, and I was grateful. During their sports games, I saw some incredible talent.

My mind was blown at the weightlifting event. I saw an athlete deadlift four hundred pounds. At the swimming competition, I met an athlete who was 80 years old and could still backstroke. She won the entire swim relay. We became great friends. Every year, I was right on the sidelines, motivating her. I felt like her personal trainer. When she finished competing, she cried and hugged me uncontrollably. She thanked me time and time again.

That day, I actually became her favorite person in the world. I didn't stop there, though. I went to every sports competition I could. I lost my voice, cheering for the athletes. I hyped the crowd up and got everybody involved. I took ownership of my work. When I saw other football players acting too cool to be involved, that's when I stepped up as a leader and told them to be more supportive of our athletes. My teammates saw how much this meant to me, so they listened and followed my lead. They went out there and had a great time.

I didn't care if you were a Division 1 (D1) athlete, a counselor, a police officer, or a person who had Down Syndrome. For me, this was about coming together and enjoying the moment. After the three-day event was over, I helped clean everything up. Everybody loves the start of the party, but it shows true passion to stay and clean up. I didn't do it for people to see how great of a person I am. I didn't do it for a medal. I did it because it's just who I am. If we all worked together, the job would get done the right way quickly.

In order for me to receive my three credit hours, I had to write a paper about my experience. I almost flunked that assignment because I avoided writing the paper. It took the coaches, academic advisor, and Jules to explain to me why I needed to sit down and write the paper. I asked Jules to correct my paper after I wrote it. She tried her best to read it back to me, but it didn't make much sense. I expected her to laugh at me and call me stupid, but she did the opposite. Jules asked me a few questions. I explained to her what I meant, and she corrected my grammar and spelling. Jules never wrote any of my papers during my time at Central Michigan. She always encouraged me to do my own work. No matter how much I begged her to write my papers, I never convinced her. I turned in my paper a week late, and I still got an A.

I couldn't wait for the Special Olympics to come around each year. I loved working with the athletes. The Special Olympics organization saw my true passion and dedication, and they awarded me with the "Spirit of Special Olympics Michigan Award." This award is for someone who models friendship, joy, acceptance, and inclusion. During the ceremony, I thanked Ms. Steely for believing in me, even when I didn't believe in myself. Ms. Steely is the true definition of a peacemaker. When you surround yourself with great people, you give yourself a chance to become even greater!

When the Detective Knocked on My Door

As I prepared to enter my sophomore year of college, dorm rooms were being assigned. I saw that I was rooming with two guys on the football team who I didn't want to be my roommates. So, I went to Ms. Steely and asked her if I could room with someone else. The school year was at capacity with students, so it was going to be hard for me to get into another room. I was on the waitlist. One of the players I was rooming with already had a bad reputation, but he didn't cause me any problems. When he was around me, he was chill and cool. I had a problem with the other roommate because he was sneaky. I needed advice on how to deal with this situation. I knew exactly who to call.

My grandma's brother, Uncle Chuck, was a disciplined man. He's an Army veteran, and he was highly respected around the city of Detroit. Uncle Chuck's speaking style is different. He often told a lot of stories to get his point across. I explained my situation with the two roommates to him. Of course, Uncle Chuck told me a story. The bottom line of that story was to let somebody know as soon as possible that I wanted to change rooms. I made another request.

I didn't have any luck with changing my room that year. After a few months passed, everything seemed cool with my roommates. So, I let my guard down. One day, as I was walking back to my door room, I saw a container filled with sand or something that looked like sand. I asked both of them what was in the container. They told me it was a science project for school. I knew one of them was lying because he never went to class. I thought maybe the coaches finally talked some sense into him, and he was actually going to class. That year, I had a Metro PCS cell phone. I'd had that cell phone since middle school, and it had finally broken. One of my boys was selling an iPhone, which was perfect timing for me. I bought it.

He was selling it for dirt cheap. Maybe it was stolen. But, at the time, I didn't care. I also bought a seven-foot fish tank. I saved a few dollars from my refund check. We couldn't have dogs, so I wanted fish. I had all types of fish in that huge fish tank, like sharks, colorful fish, and algae fish, to eat the dirt at the bottom of the tank.

My room was the chill spot. Everybody on my floor came over to my room to hang out like it was a lounge. Buying that iPhone backfired. It turned out to be stolen, and the police tracked it.

One afternoon, around 2 p.m., I was chilling in my room. I heard this big knock at the door. I saw that it was a white man in a black suit. I cracked the door slightly and asked, "How could I help you?"

He said, "We traced a stolen iPhone back to this room."

I immediately lied. I said, "There is no cell phone here."

I don't know why I lied. Honestly, I didn't think you could trace a cell phone at the time. Plus, I hadn't even turned it on yet.

The detective said, "I need to check your room."

I told him, "No." I didn't want him to find my BB gun. From time to time, during the summer, we had water balloon fights and BB gun wars. I forgot to give my BB gun to the older players who stayed off campus.

Officer Martinez, who was the on-campus police, and Officer Riley stopped over to see what was going on. I had a great relationship with Officer Martinez. I only allowed her to come into the room so we could talk. She asked me a few questions, and I told her the truth. Officer Martinez knew I wasn't a bad person. She looked out for me.

Officer Martinez said, "I can take the BB gun, but the stolen cell phone is all on you." She also told me the detective needed to come into the room to get the cell phone. The detective walked into the room with a few of his friends to look around.

I gave him the phone. That's when one of the officers yelled, "Look what we have here!" He walked into my roommates' bathroom. He said, "Mushrooms!"

I said, "Okay? They like mushrooms on their pizza! What's wrong with that?"

He said, "Mushrooms and a measuring scale."

I was confused. That's when he called the other officers into the bathroom. I didn't know what they saw, but immediately, they got on the walkie-talkie and called for backup with the dogs. They told me to sit down and get comfortable. When I say my stomach was in my underwear, I mean that literally. So many police officers and dogs raided the room. It was unreal. The other two knuckleheads weren't back in the room yet.

I couldn't explain anything. I had no clue what was going on. They blamed me for drug trafficking. Plus, the officers assumed I was growing mushrooms inside of my fish tank. Don't forget about the container I saw in the closet. Remember they said it was a school science project? It turned out to be a container to grow mushrooms. I had no idea.

I told the detective straight up, "I'm from Detroit. I know what weed looks like. I know what cocaine looks like. But I ain't never seen mushrooms a day in my life."

I thought mushrooms were legal because they go on pizza. I could tell they thought I was lying because I couldn't speak clearly. The detective said I could get up to twenty years in prison for having that type of drug in my possession. I was lightheaded after hearing that. The next day, it was all in the newspaper. This so-called drug operation made it on ESPN. It went worldwide. I got released from the football team until further notice. When I walked to class, everybody stared at me. My picture was posted all around campus. People judged me by making up stories that weren't true. One of the worst parts about being accused was that Jules' family found out.

They told her she couldn't see me anymore because I was a thug and a drug dealer. Jules tried her best to fight for me, but parents are parents. They were simply trying to protect her. Jules and I had to take a break. Every other day, the police pulled me out of class or followed me to my room. I was targeted for something I knew nothing about. I had to go to court every other week. I didn't have money for a lawyer, and my family was two hours away. I was on my own! If I developed PTSD from my childhood, just know it got worse when this issue happened.

Ms. Steely and a few others checked up on me regularly. They knew I was telling the truth. The police investigated everybody on that floor to gather as much information as they could. It was the statement of the people who hung out in our room that mattered the most. Ironically, my dorm room neighbor was a writer for the CMU newspaper. This was the same person who came into my room to hang out and party. She later wrote false accusations about us and how we were terrible roommates. In one of her articles, she mentioned the fish tank. She said she saw mushrooms growing inside the tank. Her article had a big impact on how people viewed us.

To be innocent and judged as if I was already guilty hurt the most. People treat you differently when they don't know the truth. When I say God is good, I mean *God is good*. The detective and other officers found a big notebook with all the people who were involved and who were splitting the profits from the mushrooms. My name wasn't on the list. The people who were involved told the detective that I had no part in it. During the trial, the community came to support me and spoke on my behalf about my character. Ms. Steely and a few other witnesses spoke highly of me during the trial.

Telling the judge how I tried my best to get out of that room and giving the judge proof that I was on the waiting list helped somewhat. The trial took a few days. I had to tell my side of the story. I told the truth. I didn't know anything. The judge assigned me to community service for the stolen cell phone. The detectives also caught the guy who sold me the phone. They caught him on camera stealing iPhones and laptops out of people's cars and rooms. It just happened to be one of the phones he sold me. The other two players were released from the football team and kicked out of school; they also took a plea deal.

During that time, I watched them fall apart. They blamed each other and fought a lot. I didn't understand why they chose to sell drugs. They both came from wealthy families with both parents involved. They both had promising football careers. I'm sure they would have gone to the NFL based on their talent alone. After the court hearing, they both packed up and went back to their hometowns. I never heard from them again. The coaches allowed me back on the team. But I had to miss two football games. I was so blessed that my name was cleared of all that drama. I was innocent, and I didn't want to go down for something I didn't do.

Later, the detective showed up at my door and apologized for giving me such a hard time. I knew he was only doing his job. I learned a lot throughout that whole process. I learned a valuable lesson: Never buy a cell phone off the streets without asking questions. People will judge you. But, no matter what, God sees everything. We will suffer many trials and tribulations in life. But when you keep the faith, God will help you persevere.

The Medication Fix

During my two-game suspension, I was still able to attend practices and team meetings. The first game was a few months away, and it felt good to be back on the team. You don't appreciate something until it's almost gone. I came back with a clear mindset and a fresh start. I had to meet with the coaching staff about rejoining the team. After that long meeting, the coaches also wanted to talk to me about my position status. The head coach, Dan Enos, and the other coaches thought I'd have a higher chance to play in more football games if I became a tight end.

My original position was wide receiver. Both positions do the same thing, but the tight end is mainly attached to the offensive line. At first, I got offended. I knew I needed some work, but I was most definitely capable of becoming one of the starting wide receivers. I told the coaches, "No, I'm good at switching my position." The coaches gave me some time to think about it. As we left the meeting, Coach Geno, who was the wide receiver assistant coach and now the offensive coordinator for the University of Cincinnati, pulled me to the side and told me how much of a great opportunity this could be.

He said, "With your skill set, you could be a beast at that position. Plus, the main tight end was just released."

I went back to my dorm room and weighed my options. I said to myself, "I'm barely getting playing time. I'm playing behind a superstar wideout named Titus Davis, who is a beast at wide receiver." Titus Davis started as a freshman. He was fast. He ran great routes, and, most importantly, he could catch the football really well.

Titus was for sure going to the NFL. He actually entered the draft later after three dominating seasons. He was picked up by the San Diego Chargers. Titus was the coach's favorite. I laid on my bed. I had a lot to think about. I said to myself, "I could battle this out until the end and see if I can win the coaches over, or I can gain a lot of weight and add my wide receiver skills to the tight end room and become a starter."

To be a tight end, you had to be tough and physical. You couldn't be scared to put your hand in the mud—literally. During practice, I pictured myself playing tight end. I had to make my decision before summer camp.

If playing tight end was going to give me more opportunity on the field, this was a no-brainer. I went back to the coaches with my decision and became a new member of the tight end room. Now the tight ends coach didn't play any games. He was like a drill sergeant. His name is Coach Berry. Today, he coaches for the Miami Dolphins. Coach Berry meant business! He never stopped screaming or yelling. After every football play, he ran down to his players just to scream at them, even if they did a great job. It had always been funny to me until I joined that room. I went from a luxury and exotic room with a bunch of players to a room in the basement with only four players. In the wideout room, I could get away with cracking jokes, falling asleep, and eating food. But in the basement, Coach Berry saw everything. We had to be on time and ready to learn.

You would think that after coming off suspension, I would be able to sit down, pay attention, and listen. That just wasn't the case. I tried my best to act like the other tight ends, but that's when I got in trouble the most. I couldn't stay still or focus to save my life. Coach Berry kept yelling at me like my grandma. At one point, he used the same exact words: "Deon, pay attention and stop playing so much!"

Coach Berry loved me on the field because I was a beast. I worked my butt off. But I drove him crazy in the meeting room. That's when he called my grandma to see what the problem was with me. They talked every other day. After a few days, I had to attend a meeting with Coach Berry, my grandma, and my disability teacher. They wanted me to get reevaluated. That's when the doctors diagnosed me with Attention Deficit Disorder (A.D.D.). Doctors prescribed Adderall. The medication worked somewhat, but it had some severe side effects. I was able to focus a lot more and get my work done. Also, my behavior improved greatly. Coach Berry said, "It was like night and day." When the medication wore off, though, I felt sorry for anybody that was around me. My emotions were all over the place. Some days, I was sad. Other days, I cried. And some days, I was an evil, heartless monster.

The doctors tried to find balance. In the meantime, I had to try my best to work out my problems. After a few attempts, I finally found the correct dose. Even though my behavior improved, I still struggled with the playbook. I couldn't understand the concepts or read the directions, which hurt my chances of starting that season. Even though I wrote all my papers and turned them in on time, I still needed somebody to help edit them.

I took a bunch of writing workshops. I hoped they would help me understand why I couldn't read well. My instructors were excellent, but they just couldn't seem to help me make the connection with literature. I took a few fundamentals of interpretive reading classes. I truly enjoyed those classes. I failed one with a D+, and I passed the other one with an A+. The class that I failed focused a lot on the structure of reading, like forming paragraphs and reading aloud. The other class required acting and performing.

For example, I wrote about a time in my life. Then, I performed it in front of the class. I was good at going into third-person character and making people laugh. That was the class that I passed. The instructor loved me. He told me that he taught my class for ten years and never saw anyone as good as me. I thought that was great news, but it still didn't solve my reading problem. So, I avoided classes that had a lot of writing and reading. I enrolled in more classes that required physical work, like outdoor recreation, as opposed to reading and writing. However, I soon learned that no matter what class I took, I was going to have to write a paper.

Not only did I have to work hard writing my papers, but I had to meet with two or three tutors before turning my papers in. When the tutors tried to explain to me how to structure a body paragraph, it was a foreign language to me. I didn't get to enjoy college like everybody else. My reading problems held me back from achieving my highest goals. I often felt ashamed when I was in class because of my reading issues. I wanted to learn and participate, but I was tired of running into the same problems. I asked for help.

But when I didn't get the answers I needed, it only made things more frustrating.

During football practice, I got into a lot of fights. My teammates were mad when I couldn't get the plays right. Most of the time, I started the fights due to my own frustration. It was easier to show my emotions than to tell them I couldn't read. I always had this desire to go above and beyond. But it was only so much I could do with a fourth-grade reading level. Imagine going to another country and not being able to read or speak their language. You feel lost, hopeless and shameful. That's how I felt in college. I thought the medication was going to work like a super pill and make me smarter. However, it only made me focus more. I thought college was supposed to help me gain a higher education.

I sought help, but I still couldn't find the answer to my reading problem. For the longest time, I thought I was dumb and broken. Despite the obstacles, I wasn't going to give up!

Moving My Mother into College with Me

As my sophomore year ended, I knew that meant I could no longer stay in the dorm. My grades were good, and my behavior improved significantly. The coaches approved me to move off campus. I always dreamed of having my own place and my own room since I was a little boy. This was a dream come true. I picked my roommates wisely. I needed to find a place that wasn't too far away from campus. That's when I found the perfect apartment. I signed the paperwork and got the keys. You couldn't tell me anything. I couldn't wait to organize my room or cook a home-cooked meal. I was a grown man, taking care of my own responsibilities.

This apartment was so big and impressive. I wanted my whole family to visit me and check out my new place. During the season, they didn't have to get a hotel. They could stay with me. My older brother and his friends came to visit and party often. We had some of the best times. In my new apartment, I set the rules, and it felt good. People took their shoes off at the door, and they had to clean up after themselves. When I laid on my bed, I reminisced about the time I created a bedroom in the closet when I lived with my grandma.

I thanked God for blessing me with my own place. I was excited to go back home to visit my grandma and mother. I wanted to share the good news about my new apartment. But when I went back home, my mother looked a mess. I felt sad because I was doing so well, yet they were struggling. When I sat down to talk with my grandma, I could feel her pain. She was tired of the family drama. My grandma needed a break. I wanted to help, but I didn't know how. So, I asked my mother to come live with me for a few months. I thought maybe if she stayed with me, she would get off drugs and get a job. When I drove back to school, I packed my mother up and took her with me. My roommates were fine with my mother staying with us for a while.

The apartment was so big that they wouldn't even notice if she was there or not. Plus, we were always at practices or in class. Like any king of the house, I told her, "Mi casa es su casa." In other words, my house was her house! My teammates and friends loved having my mom around the house because she cooked some good food and was a cool person to hang around with. My mother cleaned the apartment, and she took care of my fish tank.

However, my mom smoked a lot of cigarettes. I hated cigarettes because I knew what they do to the lungs. I tried to help her quit. However, I learned that some people smoked cigarettes to calm their nerves. I heard stories from my siblings that my mom had a rough childhood. I never took that into consideration. I never asked my mom about her past. I was too afraid to remember my *own* past and trauma. So, I stayed away from touchy topics and did my best to focus on the good moments. Many days, my mother helped me with my schoolwork. She was smart and intelligent at math. She also knew how to write papers.

I often walked into the apartment after a long day of practice and caught my mother writing goals for herself. She had a book full of ideas she wanted to accomplish. Some days, I came back to the apartment and saw Jules and my mother watching movies together. I had my own mini family in college. My mother told me, "You better do right by Jules because she is a good one."

My mother witnessed firsthand the side effects of my medication. She didn't like that side of me. I sometimes disrespected Jules by the way I spoke to her. My mother would say to me, "Don't think you're too old and big for a butt whooping." It felt good to see my mother smiling and happy again. She truly looked like her normal self. She was full of love and joy. I wanted her to stay forever, but she was soon ready to go back home.

She went back to Inkster and got a house and a job. She lived a few blocks away from my grandma. My dad and brothers moved back in with my mom, and things were back on track. Once again, my grandma had her house to herself and was back being sarcastic and funny.

When building a strong foundation, sometimes you have to watch and learn. All my life, I watched my grandma sacrifice her life to build the perfect family. I never saw my grandma ask for help. When I saw that she was tired from all the stress, she didn't need to ask me for help. I already knew my role. When I went back to school, I didn't show up empty-handed. I went back with a newborn puppy, and I named him Ace.

Moving My Little Brother Into College With Me

My apartment complex didn't allow dogs, so I kept Ace at Jules' apartment. I got Ace certified as a service dog because of my mental health issues. In the meantime, I had to look for a different apartment that allowed dogs. I found one that accepted pit bulls. Ace became my best friend. I truly needed him in my life. Anytime you saw me, you saw Ace. Everybody loved Ace in the community. I even brought Ace to football practice with me during bring-your-child-to-work day. The coaches actually thought it was a clever idea. All the coaches' kids got to play with Ace. The new season was getting ready to start, and I wanted to go home one last time so my grandma could meet Ace.

Once I arrived at my grandma's house, I saw the neighborhood full of police. Cops were everywhere. When I asked my grandma what happened, she said, "A little boy just got killed." I checked Facebook because that's where I knew I could get information and updates. I found out it was my little brother DeMarco's best friend. That's when I went to my mother's house to check up on my little brother. Marco was crying in disbelief. It was hard seeing my brother in pain. It was also sad to know that his best friend had been murdered.

His name was Wayy. He was the coolest kid on the block. Wayy was a good soul. He was very quiet, and he stayed to himself. He was simply at the wrong place at the wrong time. Somebody started shooting, and he was the one who got shot. I called my coaches to let them know that I needed to stay a few more days at home. My little brother needed me. The people in the city of Inkster were torn up about Wayy's death. He was an innocent kid who had a bright future. A big gang war broke out. It was a scary time for anybody to be outside. At one point, the SWAT team had to get involved. I knew my brother wasn't okay. Marco meant business. I wasn't about to allow his emotions to get the best of him. I didn't want him to make a decision that was going to cost him a lifetime in prison.

So, I packed up everything he owned, and I put it in the back of my truck. Then, I told him we were going out to eat. What he didn't know was that I was taking him back to school with me. I had already talked with my mother and grandma about this idea, and they both agreed this would be best. Marco fought me the whole way back to school. He hated me! Once we arrived at my apartment, he went into the room, and he didn't talk to me for a while. He didn't eat for a week.

When I talked to my friends back home, they told me the city was out of control. A few more people got killed, and a few people went to prison. I didn't care if Marco hated me. He'd just had a newborn baby. I wanted him to be in his child's life. If making a decision like that meant him hating me for a while, so be it. Marco started talking to Ace before he started talking to me. That was a good sign. I gave Marco my apartment while I stayed at Jules's place. Eventually, Marco thanked me for getting him to see the bigger picture. Later, he asked me if his baby's mother and son could move into the apartment with him. I agreed.

Marco loved being in Mount Pleasant. I introduced him to all the coaches and players. My teammates loved him like he was a part of the family. Marco was exposed to the college lifestyle. Having Marco around made me feel good. I said to him one day, "How cool would it be if you became a college student?" That's when I enrolled him in a community college. The community college was right up the street from CMU. Marco adapted to the college lifestyle quickly. He made new friends and also got good grades. But then, we ran into a problem.

I warned Marco about his refund check. I told him to save his money because it could be gone in a blink of an eye. We don't come from a family of money. I learned from experience. He looked me right in the face and said, "Trust me. I'm going save my refund check." I reminded him every single day before he received his check to save it. I did my best to give him guidance. Due to my busy schedule, we needed a routine. I had to drop him off and pick him up every day from school. Jules and my roommates also helped me out. Mount Pleasant was known for Soaring Eagle Casino. It was nice for college students because you only needed to be eighteen to get in the doors.

After my class was over, I went to pick him up at his regular spot. However, he wasn't there. I thought maybe he had a test or something. I waited in the parking lot. I called him a few times, but his phone went right to voicemail. I thought maybe he had caught a ride home and forgot to tell me. I went back to the apartment and asked my roommates if they saw my brother. They hadn't. I was praying that he wasn't stranded somewhere with a dead phone. I started to get worried. Then, I realized he was probably at the casino.

Unfortunately, I was right. He was sitting at the craps table, looking crazy. The look on his face said everything. I walked over to him, but he didn't say a word to me. I asked him, "How much did you lose?"

He replied, "The whole thing."

I said, "The whole refund check?"

I felt so bad for him because he was only trying to support his family. He thought he could use his refund money by gambling to win more money. I pulled out a hundred dollars to see if I could help win some of his money back. The casino took that faster than I could raise my hand.

Once we got into the car, he lost control. His emotions exploded. He started beating my dashboard. He was crying and screaming, and there was nothing I could do for him. He had lost $2,500. I felt horrible, so I gave him $300. I told him not to blow the money this time. He looked at me with those puppy eyes and said, "Thank you." He most definitely learned his lesson because he held on to that $300 until he went back to Detroit. My grandma showed me that family should always look out for one another.

Today, my little brother is doing really well. He has a beautiful family. He's a mentor and also a basketball coach. Sometimes, you have to experience something yourself to learn a valuable lesson. But there's a difference between the people who want to be great and the people who are okay with being average. When you want to be great, you learn from other people's mistakes. You learn as much as you can and as fast as you can. The people who are okay with being average will only listen after they repeat the same mistake. You also need to know from who to take advice. Everybody doesn't have your best interest at heart. It's important to be aware of the people you allow to influence you.

Life In Prison

My whole life, I've felt that I was the one who was meant for prison. I couldn't read. I had trouble with spelling. I was kicked out of school every week for fighting. People considered me to be the troubled child. My older brother was the one everybody praised. They thought he was going to be the golden child. Lawrence was an honor roll student, and he was everybody's favorite. Now, he's facing life in prison without parole. It was the beginning of my junior year in college. Football was finally going my way. The coaches were learning to trust me on the football field. My grades looked really good.

One day after practice, my mother called me to tell me my older brother Lawrence was in jail again. But this time, I wasn't shocked. Earlier that year, my grandma told me this was going to happen. During preseason, I went home to bond Lawrence out of jail. He was pulled over without a driver's license. I had to hustle up some money from my friends and high school coaches. I drove to the police station. That's when I was able to free him the first time. As we sat in the parking lot of the police station, we talked in the car. Lawrence said he was going to get his life together. I believed him! Later that night, I went to my grandma's house.

I went off on my entire family for not helping me get him home from jail. My grandma calmed me down. I was enraged. She talked to me in a peaceful tone. My grandma said, "You have a big heart and you mean well. But you just don't understand certain things." I was confused. My family always told me we were always supposed to stick together, especially in times of need. My grandma said, "Sometimes people need to learn their lesson and sit down." That was hard for me to hear because my brother and I were close.

When my mother called me about him going to jail again, she said, "This time, he doesn't have a bond amount." He needed a lawyer. This was serious. A lawyer was going to be impossible for us to afford. My family wouldn't tell me what he did. Everybody wanted me to focus on football and school, but that was hard to do, especially knowing that my older brother and older cousin were facing life in prison. I come from the streets, so I wasn't oblivious to the facts about violence. My older cousin was a good man. He took care of his family, but he also didn't play any games. So, when I learned they both faced life in prison, I already knew it had something to do with murder.

I knew my cousin had it in him to kill, but not my brother. Lawrence couldn't kill a fly with his eyes open. However, peer pressure and fear mixed together can make a person do the unthinkable. When Lawrence went to trial, he had a court-appointed lawyer. The judge first offered him a plea deal, with 10-15 years in prison. Lawrence felt like he didn't deserve that much time in prison, so he turned that deal down. He wanted to fight the case, so he took his chances in trial. For me, this was the worst feeling in the world. No one told me anything. I tried following his case. But when you can't read well, it's hard to research anything. My cousin went to trial and was sentenced to 40-60 years in prison right away. He'd beat a murder case before, but not this time. I was lost for words because I loved my cousin. I looked up to him.

My cousin could be a scary man to others. But, to me, he tried his best. He respected me a lot because he knew I didn't fear him. He also knew I took care of my family. No matter what people say about him, deep down, he was a good man who was trying to survive in the jungle. My brother's trial took two months. They investigated him in-depth and found him guilty of accessory to murder. The judge gave my older brother life in prison.

My heart was broken in disbelief. Imagine trying so hard to keep your family together, and every time you make progress, something bigger goes wrong. This causes your family to separate even more. No matter how hard I tried, I felt like I couldn't get anything right. I couldn't make Lawrence's trial, but I remember my mother calling me crying and hurt about his case. I hated hearing the pain in my mother's voice. I felt her heart sinking over the phone. I couldn't even imagine what she was feeling as a mother. Her son was about to do life in prison, and there was nothing she could do about it.

My brother went to prison at the age of twenty-four. I tried my best, but there was nothing I could do. I thought about his son and daughter. They were going to have to grow up without a father in their lives. This is the consequence of not thinking about your actions while only living in the moment. The people around you also get hurt and suffer the consequences. It was a sad time for my family. I looked online, and I saw a picture of my brother. He had his head down with handcuffs on. I honestly couldn't imagine what was running through his head at the time. What I do know is he was about to do life in prison for being around the wrong people.

I was there when God gave my brother so many wake-up calls, chance after chance. God sent angel after angel, message after message. But when you are going down the wrong path and following the way of weakness, you tend to miss God's message the most. Life can be hard sometimes, especially when you're trying to provide for a better future. Always remember that shortcuts in life only lead to destruction. The longer path might seem a bit challenging, but I promise you it will be worth it. There's a reason you need to master every step you take in life.

I Make Mistakes, Too

Of course, when my brother got life in prison, it was a distraction for me. But I couldn't stop my life because I was so close to achieving something I thought was impossible. During the summer, I took my leadership skills to a whole different level. I memorized the playbook, and I also stayed in the weight room. I took the young players under my belt, and I taught them everything I knew. I took a few summer classes. So, when it was time to graduate, I wasn't behind.

Summer camp was coming up, and we had two weeks to prepare for the Gasher Test. The Gasher Test is where you have to run half of the football field in a certain amount of time. Each position group had to run twenty times. Every player had to pass their conditioning test. If we failed, we had to redo it until we passed. This test either made you or broke you. In my opinion, you had to be a beast to pass it on the first try. I trained with Jason Wilson, who was my roommate, and Martez Walker, who was like my little brother. We trained for the Gasher Test almost every day.

One day after working out, I invited a few players over to my place for a cookout.

I loved grilling food. So, during the summer, I hosted a lot of cookouts. But sometimes, things got out of control. My teammate Louis, who played defensive tackle, joined the cookout. Louis and I were both from Detroit. We always talked about how we had to protect ourselves growing up in the hood. Louis knew a lot about guns. He could name every type of gun. Big Lue was his nickname, and he asked to see my gun. When I showed him my weapon, he named parts I knew nothing about. Once Big Lue finished analyzing my 9mm, he gave it back to me. I pointed the gun at him, even though it wasn't loaded. This is where things got out of control. Big Lue told me not to play like that. Like my grandma always said, "I needed to learn when to play and not to play."

At that moment, I started playing too much! I kept pointing my gun at Big Lue, and I told him to stop crying. He asked me a few more times to stop, but I refused to take him seriously. That's when he walked over to me and sized me up. We faced off. He had beast mode in his eyes. Of course, I switched right into beast mode, as well. If you ever saw two lions in the jungle sizing each other up, that's how we looked at the time.

I wasn't backing down. Neither was Big Lue. Martez and Jason jumped into the middle of us to break us apart. That day, Big Lue and I stopped being friends. Every time we walked past each other, we wanted to kill one another. This small situation turned out to be a big problem. The coaches and the players had to keep us apart. This issue divided the whole team. The defense of players sided with Big Lue, and the offense of players sided with me, no matter who was right or wrong. Big Lue had that name for a reason. He was about 6' 2" and weighed two hundred and seventy pounds. I didn't care because I have the heart of a lion. Even though I was a great leader to the rest of the team, deep down, I didn't feel good about myself when it came down to Big Lue. I knew I was wrong, but my pride got the best of me. God kept telling me that I needed to fix this problem.

It was time for our Gasher Test. The weather didn't help. It was like ninety degrees outside, which made our conditioning test much harder. I didn't care about how hot it was outside. I was overly prepared to win this test. A few players who came back from summer break weren't so lucky. They suffered tremendously because they were out of shape. They complained a lot as we ran through hell.

This was my time to shine. I ran as hard as I could every time my group had to run. I needed to be first. I wanted my teammates to know that I was the hardest worker on the team. After I completed my test, I motivated the other players to finish strong. I had a great start in camp. This was my year. I also had my eyes on being voted team captain. After building a strong relationship over time with Coach Berry, who was my position coach, he became the offensive line coach. I was upset because I didn't do well with change. Then, the head coach, Dan Enos, hired Sherrone Moore from Oklahoma to be our tight ends coach.

Coach Moore seemed like a cool guy, but I wasn't about to let him walk in our meeting room and run the show. He needed to earn my trust. I immediately tested him. The first few days of camp, I gave Coach Moore a hard time. I wanted to see if Coach Moore could handle the pressure. Right away, he called me out and made me sit in the front-row seat in our meeting room. I tried everything in my power to make him mad and frustrated. However, he stood strong. He could withstand the pressure.

Coach Moore pulled me to the side like a real father and said, "No matter what you try, no matter how hard you try to push me away, I want you to know that I'll never give up on you." At that moment in my life, I heard God speak through another person. Not only did he say it, but he meant every word. From that point on, I trusted Coach Moore. I took ownership of what I was passionate about, and I didn't let anything get in my way. I made some big plays at practice. I was blocking until the whistle was blown. I caught every pass that was thrown my way. I scored numerous touchdowns. I also made tackles on special teams. I didn't have any room for mistakes.

Each year during camp, it was a tradition for all the seniors to give a speech. All the seniors stuck to the traditional way and talked about their time at CMU. When it was my time, I wanted it to be special. So, I stood up in front of all the coaches and players, and I dedicated my senior speech to Big Lue. I apologized to him face to face. I asked him for his forgiveness. This was one of the hardest things I had to do. But it was the *right* thing to do. I cried as I looked Big Lue right in his eyes. Then, I apologized.

He saw that I was sincere. He gave me a hug, and he forgave me. That's when we both put our hate for one another behind us. I learned a few things during that moment. First, it's okay to apologize when you're wrong. I'm not perfect, and I make mistakes. Second, doing the right thing feels uncomfortable, but it's better than holding a grudge. Last, it's okay for men to cry. Being tough all the time is just a show. I felt so much better after I apologized. During that time, the coaches and players all stood up and started clapping. Everybody was excited. They saw growth in both of us. The meeting room was filled with so much joy! Nobody knew why we were fighting, but only the few players who were at the cookout. I knew the truth, and I saw how this affected our team.

Hate, anger, pride, and ego are the downfall of a person's success. It's hard to apologize, but it's even harder to accept someone's apology. This is how I knew Big Lue was a good man. He accepted my apology, even though he did nothing wrong. This was an epic moment for the team!

God will help you in your toughest moments. All we have to do is humble ourselves and listen. Later, during camp, the team voted. I didn't win team captain. A. G., who played running back, gave a heroic speech about how he was going to change his attitude and become more of a team player. Yes! I was salty that I didn't win.

My energy was low during practices and meetings because I really had my mind set on becoming team captain. That's when Coach Moore stepped in and said something that sparked flames back into my soul.

"You don't need to be the team captain to be a great leader!" What Coach Moore said to me that day meant the world to me. My attitude went from poor to greatness. My mindset went to a whole different level. Sometimes, when we don't get what we want, we get bitter or become negative. But if we truly trust in God, we will soon see that He has a better plan in mind.

This was my best camp over the course of four years. I was more comfortable on the field because I memorized the whole playbook. Coach Moore noticed that I was struggling with the audibles. An audible is when the quarterback makes an adjustment at the last minute after the original play is called. For example, Cooper Rush would say, "44 west!" twice at the line of scrimmage. I would panic and go the wrong way or make the wrong block. I didn't know my east from west. After practice, Coach Moore called me to his office.

He asked, "Do you know your east from west?"

I hesitated. I told him the truth. "No, I don't know my east from west."

Once again, I started crying. I was so embarrassed that I couldn't read, nor did I know my left from right. I told Coach Moore the truth because I was so tired of fighting with myself. This problem had been tormenting me my entire life. I expected Coach Moore to laugh at me, like people in my past. He did the opposite.

He gave me a hug and said, "I got you."

Coach Moore gave me a few key pointers that helped me remember the audibles. Coach Moore said, "When you hear west, it rhymes with left. East is the opposite of left." This was the best method ever to help me remember. I went from getting ninety percent of the plays right to getting a hundred percent of the plays right.

I felt very confident about the playbook. During our meetings, I was able to use different color markers on the whiteboard. I was able to tell stories to help me learn the plays faster. This elevated my game to another level. I started my senior year. That was a great moment for me because I knew the coaches had full trust in me. We had a great start to the season. We played Purdue, which is a Big Ten School, and we beat them 38-17. We went crazy in the locker room. You would've thought we won the Super Bowl by the way we were acting.

This is why the coaches preach to stay humble. The next game, we played Syracuse, and they punched us right in the mouth. We lost 40-3. In that game, the coaches looked for me to step it up and make some big plays. I just couldn't get my engine going. A few games passed, and our season looked terrible. We had just lost three straight games. A few of our key players were out due to injuries, such as our superstar running back, Thomas Ross, who later played for the Seattle Seahawks. Our seniors had a team meeting with just seniors. We needed to step up our game and turn this season around. We did just that. We practiced harder and played better.

I made big plays, and everybody else stepped up their game. Key players came back, and we won more games. What I learned during our losing streak was that people only love you when you are winning. We had to block out the outside noise and trust the process. When we were losing, everybody gave up on us. But, as a team, we stuck together and trusted each other. Then, we won games. Our fans started loving us again.

Graduating from College Reading at a Fourth Grade Level

chool was going really well for me. I needed a few more credits in order to graduate. The fall semester of my junior year, I got a 3.0 GPA. This was my last year in college. I wanted to aim higher, so I did everything I could to get better grades. I studied every single day. I went to all my classes and met with all my tutors. I talked to all my professors after class just to make sure that I understood the work. That's when I ran into a problem with one of my professors. I was failing her class. When I scheduled a meeting with her, that's when I realized why I was failing. During our meeting, I showed her that I needed special accommodations with my schoolwork. However, she refused to help me or believe me.

She said, "Because you're a football player, you think you deserve special treatment."

Parents and loved ones, this is why it's so important to know that knowledge is power. I wanted to tell somebody about this issue, but I didn't know who to tell or how to report it. At first, this professor didn't allow me to see my disability teacher. Then, she made me take my exams and tests with the entire class. When I raised my hand in class, she overlooked me. I did everything I could to pass this class. But this professor had something against me … or maybe against football players in general. I ended up failing that class with a D+. In all my other classes, I got A's. I busted my butt. I went above and beyond. I had to put in overtime work because I couldn't read or spell well. This made my college experience so much more difficult. My GPA ended up being a 2.8. I was hurt that semester, but I did all I could do. At that time, I was satisfied. Looking back on it, I was cutting myself short. When you are aiming to achieve something in life, when you are the one putting in the hard work, you deserve to be rewarded. Don't ever settle for less.

In the meantime, we won football games and fought hard to make a bowl game. To do so, we first needed to beat Buffalo. Before the game started, I felt like something was wrong. I didn't know what, though. I ended up having the best game of my career. I blocked great. I caught every football that was thrown my way. It was the fourth quarter, and we needed a first down to win the game. I made the game-winning catch! The players, the coaches, and the crowd went crazy with excitement. We went into the locker room with so much passion, knowing that we were bowl-eligible. That's when I checked my phone and found out my Uncle Redd had passed away.

I was hurt. My spirit crashed. I was sick to my stomach. I blacked out. I was an emotional wreck in the locker room. I couldn't believe another one of my grandma's kids had just overdosed from drugs. I talked to my grandma, and, of course, her heart was broken. I tried to do everything to get back home, but my grandma wanted me to stay at school. She knew I didn't do well with funerals. I missed my favorite uncle's funeral. I didn't even get a chance to say, "Goodbye." I missed football practice for a week, and I didn't go to class. I went into a dark place with a chip on my shoulder. I had pain in my eyes, and somebody needed to pay.

That's when I decided to release everything I had into my final season. The coaches saw that I meant business and I wasn't taking names. I dominated. I elevated my game. My teammates were very supportive when my uncle passed away, but they also saw the fire in my eyes. So, they followed my lead. The next game, we were playing Eastern Michigan. We blew them out 38-7. I had an explosive game. I smashed players—literally. As a team, we connected on both sides of the ball. The defense played great football, and our offense couldn't be stopped. After the game, I received the game-winning ball. I had seven catches for ninety-five yards.

There was one more game left until my senior year was over. It was against our rival, Western Michigan. If you lived in Mount Pleasant and missed this game, it had better be for a great reason: everybody knew both teams' history. We didn't like them, and they didn't like us—respectfully! The best part was that we played them at our house, Kelly Stadium. This was a great way to end my senior season. The team was pumped. I looked out the doors before the game started. I saw the whole stadium filled with fans and family members. You couldn't hear anything because it was so loud. The weather was perfectly sunny with clear skies.

The game started at 1 p.m. Before the game started, the captains went out for the coin toss. Something happened because our head coach, Dan Enos, came back into the locker room, tripping out and yelling about something. I was in the other room meditating when Coach Enos suddenly called a team meeting. He was furious with anger! I thought this was his way of getting us ready for the game, but he started yelling at our captains. During the coin toss, they didn't show good sportsmanship. Western Michigan captains decided to kick the ball instead of receiving the ball. Once Western Michigan made their decision, they went in for a handshake out of respect.

Our captains turned their backs on them and walked away. Before the coin toss took place, a few of our captains agreed not to shake their hands. What our captains didn't know was that we'd just added fuel to their fire. We also got fined $10,000. Coach Enos pulled me to the side and told me, "Take the lead right now!"

I looked him in his eyes and said, "Yes, sir!" I came out and scored the first touchdown. The crowd went nuts. I ended up having seven catches for eighty-three yards.

We played well, but not good enough to win. Western Michigan didn't back down. They must have taken that handshake thing personally. We needed that win to play in the MAC championship. Instead, we had to settle for a bowl game. Little did we know that this bowl game was better than playing in the MAC championship. This bowl game was about to change our lives forever! The whole team thought we were playing in the Quick Lane Bowl game, which is a bowl game hosted by Detroit. There wasn't anything wrong with that bowl game.

We had already played in that bowl game two years ago. But we ended up being picked to play in the Bahamas Bowl. This caught us by surprise. We jumped out of our seats when we heard the news. This was a great way to end my college career, but it got even better. Before the bowl game, I was about to do something I couldn't even imagine. I was about to get my college degree. When I received the email that I was walking across the stage on December 13, 2014, I called my grandma with excitement.

"Look, granny! We did it. I did the unexpected! Thank you for believing in me and pushing me to the limit."

This was much better than buying her a house or gifting her with a car. I did something on my side of the family that no one thought was possible. I give thanks to God and my family for supporting me. My grandma was too ill to show up for my graduation, but my mother, dad, Aunt Diane, and Vanessa supported me. We had a great time. When I looked into the stands, it was the best feeling seeing my family cheering my name—not for sports—but for something I did educationally. I saw how happy my mother was for me. She cried as she cheered. My teammate L. T. Walton, who played defensive tackle, had the exact graduation date and time as I did. So, we spent time together during the ceremony.

L. T. was also from Detroit. He was trying to make a way for his family. We had a few celebratory shots of tequila before walking across the stage. When they called our names, we did a little celebration dance as we walked to receive our degrees. Afterward, I went out to eat with my parents. I remembered them dropping me off for college. Now, they were picking me up from college. It's crazy how life works and how time flies. At first, I couldn't imagine myself going to college. I'd just received my degree, all while reading at a fourth-grade level.

God is truly good. I felt so blessed. It was weird going to football practices without any college classes. I felt free as an eagle.

The Bahamas Bowl Game

We stayed at the Atlantis Paradise Island. We were in for the time of our lives. Even though we needed to stay focused, we still wanted to have fun. We played Western Kentucky University, and they were the real deal. At the time, they were the number one offense in their conference. It was hard trying to stay focused with all this excitement around us. I had a fantastic time. I got to swim with dolphins and also meet Magic Johnson.

I learned a lot about the people on the island and the different tribes. There was a big parade going on, and it was amazing. I love dancing and having a good time, so I joined their parade. I see why they call it Paradise Island. The bowl game was in two days. We were about to be in for a huge surprise. This game meant a lot for us because one of our teammates was battling cancer. Derek Nash had a sad story. He played running back and he was one of the greatest football players I ever witnessed. Unfortunately, D. Nash's cancer caused his season to end early. We watched D. Nash battle all season with cancer. It was hard seeing somebody so young fight against something they couldn't control.

The doctors told D. Nash he was too sick to take the trip to The Bahamas, but D. Nash refused that advice. He told the doctors that this was his time to shine and be with his family. He dreamed of this moment his whole life. He was not about to allow anything to get in his way. Football made D. Nash extremely happy, even with all that was going on in his life. He still managed to smile and cheer others up. You couldn't tell he had cancer because he was always in a great mood. He kept a smile on his face. He always joked around.

I think D. Nash knew his time was short. After the bowl game, he passed away. I'm so happy that D. Nash didn't quit on his dreams. We gave him a show he couldn't forget. D. Nash didn't ask for much. The only thing he wanted from us was that we "played for him and prayed for him." On the day of the game, the weather was unbelievably hot. The grass was dry, and it felt like we were playing in a desert. As soon as the game started, Western Kentucky came out and scored the first touchdown.

You would've thought this was going to be a boxing match because we came right back at them with a touchdown by Titus Davis. But Western Kentucky wasn't playing any games. They scored touchdowns every time they touched the football. You can tell our defense was feeling the heat from the sun because they were gassed out. Western Kentucky took full advantage of the weather. Going into halftime, the score was 42-14. This is not how I pictured my senior season ending. Once we entered the locker room, the seniors spoke up and motivated the team.

I paused for a moment. I reflected on all the challenges that I faced in my life. This was the easiest one to figure out. I didn't care about the scoreboard. We just needed to put up a fight. The leadership in me took over in the locker room. I spoke powerful energy into the offense. I also noticed the captains on the defense speaking very passionately with a lot of emotion. This game was far from over. We came out of halftime with a different mindset. The goal was to catch Western Kentucky sleeping as if they already won the game. We needed to do the little things that mattered the most. We had to do the things that made the team stronger physically, mentally and emotionally.

I learned over the years that the team that had the most momentum usually won the game. We were the underdogs with nothing to lose. It was our ball coming out of half-time. It was third in fifteen. We needed this first down. Cooper Rush, who is now the quarterback for the Dallas Cowboys, threw the football to me. I dove at least ten yards to get the first down. This was just to get the team going. After I made that catch, I looked over to my teammates with so much enthusiasm and energy. That catch I made fired up the running backs. Saylor, Devin, and AG woke up.

But it was Martez Walker, out of the running backs, who took ownership in running the football. I knew Martez very well. I pulled him to the side and pumped energy into his ear. Martez instantly went into beast mode, which led to Titus Davis scoring another touchdown. I watched Cody Lopez and Justin Cherocci, who played defensive linebackers, take full control in stopping Western Kentucky's powerful run game. This gave our offense more possessions. Then, the wide receivers elevated their game. Courtney Davis, Jesse Kroll and Anthony Rice caught everything. Titus scored another touchdown. We played like a team that didn't care about winning or losing. The goal was to put up a fight, and that's what we did.

The defense had just caused a major fumble, which led to Courtney Davis' touchdown. Special teams and the defense played the biggest role in our comeback. Then Anthony, who played running back, scored a touchdown. Before we knew it, the score was 42 to 49. We kicked the ball off to Western Kentucky. We needed one more stop from the defense. This was asking a lot, but I knew it could be done. The crowd got loud. The sideline made noise, and the coaches were fired up. The defense deserves a lot of credit for stopping this powerfully ranked offense from getting a first down. Western Kentucky had to punt the ball back to us, which left one second on the clock. Talk about the angels being on our side. It was time for a one-second Hail Mary play. This had to be the craziest play ever.

We were about to make history from this Hail Mary play. Cooper Rush hiked the ball, and he did everything he could to give us time to run down the field. That's when Cooper threw up a prayer pass to Jesse Kroll. Jesse jumped in the air and came down with the football. He had two defensive players on his back. Jesse and I locked eyes. That's when he pitched me the football. Once I got the ball, for a minute, I thought that I could've been the player who won the game because I saw nothing but the end zone.

I took off running with the ball as fast as I could. However, I noticed five of the defensive players surrounding me. I turned into a grenade and drew them all to me. As I was tackled to the grass, I pitched the ball to Courtney Davis. Because I was left-handed, this worked out perfectly. Courtney drew three more players to himself, then pitched the ball to Titus Davis. That's when Titus took off running with the football. For a minute, he didn't look like he was going to make it into the end zone because he had a few players on his tail. Titus turned into Superman and dove at least five yards into the end zone. Everybody paused and watched the referee throw his hands into the air as he called for a touchdown! The score was now 48-49. After that big comeback, we felt like we had the momentum. We decided to go for a two-point conversion.

A lot of our fans thought we should've gone for the extra point to go into overtime. But we were tired, hot, and drained. There was no way we were going to survive in overtime with this great team we were up against. This was not the coach's decision; this was a team decision. So, we went for the two-point conversion and didn't get it. Western Kentucky beat us in The Bahamas Bowl. They won the game, but we won the war. Every sports channel was talking about us.

Western Kentucky looked depressed after they won the game. This bowl game was nominated for the best comeback game of the year. That Hail Mary play went down in history. I learned that it's not about how you start but how you finish. We kept fighting, and we kept our spirits up. We didn't stop believing, and we kept our faith. Because of that, we did the unthinkable. What a great way to end my senior season! I walked off the field with my head held high, knowing that I gave it my all. Going to college didn't just get me my education or a full-ride scholarship to play football. It opened a new pathway of hope for the future. I thank God, my grandma, family, coaches, and mentors who helped me during this journey to greatness. I talked with the team before I said my goodbyes. I wanted them to know that life is full of challenges. But when you believe and persevere through the good and bad times, no matter what, you will become a winner. I want to dedicate this chapter to Derek Nash and Titus Davis, who are no longer with us. May God continue to bless you and your families.

Nobody's bigger than the team.

The NFL (Not For Long)

The NFL draft was coming up. My head coach, Dan Enos, called me to his office. He told me the NFL was interested in my talent. I had a chance to play football at the next level. I didn't believe him until a few NFL scouts visited me during my winter training at Central Michigan University. Since I was a little boy, I always dreamed of playing in the NFL. Growing up, I was so excited to tell my family members and friends that I was going to play in the NFL one day. They didn't believe me. People often told me, "You're not going to the NFL. You can't even read."

They always told me that I was dreaming too big. So, when NFL scouts actually recruited me, it felt unreal. But I knew one person who believed in my dreams; my grandma. I couldn't wait to call her to tell her that I might have a chance to play at the next level. All thirty-two teams were interested in me. However, six teams were highly interested in me, the Detroit Lions being one of them. When I would finish meeting with NFL coaches, the first thing I thought about was how I could buy my grandma a house.

The second thing I thought about was how I could take care of the rest of my family. After talking with my grandma and sharing the good news, I sensed the smile on her face. I felt the release of hope for a better future. The business side of football got serious. Due to my value in football, I needed to sign with an NFL agent. This was the scariest part of the business. I'd heard negative stories about NFL agents. They would use players for their money, steal from them, and take advantage of the players just to get ahead.

I was very careful about who I chose to be my agent. I interviewed nine guys and one lady. These agents did their best to sell themselves to me, but I was smart when I was making my decision. I needed somebody who was going to work hard for me, not just see me as a cash cow. I needed somebody who had true passion for their craft and a big heart like my grandma. I needed somebody who was going to work day and night for me. When it came down to football, I wasn't the fastest player or the strongest player. I needed somebody who was going to help me stand out. I signed with a woman agent, which was unusual at that time.

People didn't think women knew much about football. But I looked at it from a different perspective. Picking a female agent was one of my best decisions. My agent's name was Alisa. She was like a mother away from home. Alisa worked her tail off for me. Her work ethic was unreal, and she had the biggest heart. During my training sessions, Alisa checked up on me to make sure I stayed focused. She paid for things out of her own pocket and also made sure that I took in all the proper nutrition. If you are somebody who's thinking about playing in the NFL, it's super important that you pick the right agent. You don't need a big-time agent who won't focus on all your wants and needs. Just know that your talent alone will get you noticed.

At the beginning of 2015, I traveled a lot. I was blessed to be a part of the 2015 Sports Science Award and the ESPYs. I had a great time. I got to experience a whole different side of the world and meet some of my favorite athletes and comedians, like Marshawn Lynch, Aaron Rogers, Odell Beckham, Michael Blackson, and Kevin Hart. It was amazing meeting all these superstars, but the best part about being in Los Angeles was meeting up with Crystal Bradford.

Crystal was the first African-American woman to be drafted in the WNBA coming out of Central Michigan University. Crystal and I went to the same high school and college together. We both grew up in the ghetto of Detroit and Inkster. Imagine our energy when we saw each other out in California! We were overly excited. It was amazing seeing another person from the hood who battled hard to overcome adversity. I invited Crystal and her friends to come party with me at this fancy club. I didn't have any money at the time, but I did have Marshawn Lynch, who invited me to the party. Marshawn Lynch played for the Seattle Seahawks in the NFL. He was known for being one of the best running backs to ever play.

Financially, Marshawn took care of everything. He looked out for me. When I first got around Marshawn Lynch and his friends, I wanted to act like I had all this money. I wanted to act like I was this big-time baller. But I was lying to myself just to fit in with the crowd. Marshawn pulled me to the side and told me to just be myself. He promised me he was going to take care of everything. Throughout my life, my grandma, coaches, and mentors told me that character is everything. When Marshawn pulled me to the side, he showed me the true definition of having good character.

Afterward, we partied on the rooftop and ate some really good food. I enjoyed my time with Crystal and everybody else who joined us that night. The next day, I got a duffle bag full of gifts to travel all around the world from the ESPYs. That bag had all types of free trips to different islands and different states. What truly blew my mind was seeing an Uber Jet gold card in the bag. This jet would've picked us up from the airport and taken us to any island. On the day of The ESPYs, we were nominated for the best play. However, we came in as runner-up against Odell

Beckham, who made a one-handed catch for the New York Giants. I'm still thankful for that amazing experience.

I went back home, excited about all the potential opportunities. But I still had a lot of training left for the NFL Pro Day. Pro Day is the day that all thirty-two teams in the NFL get to watch you train and perform drills. Depending on your test results, you get drafted or even noticed to play at the next level. Not only do they test your body, but also your mind. This test is called The Wonderlic Test. Because I couldn't read well, this test gave me anxiety before I could actually work out physically in front of the NFL scouts. I sat there, looking at that test, full of fear. There was no way I was going to make it to the NFL because of my reading issues.

During Pro Day, I didn't have the best test results. But I did work my butt off. Unfortunately, I didn't get drafted. However, I did sign with the Detroit Lions that year. Talk about a blessing from God! Me and Jules were in Cincinnati at her apartment, watching the draft. I paid close attention during the seventh round. That is when I was projected to get drafted. When I didn't hear my name called during the 2015 NFL draft, my stomach rolled over. I was so disappointed that I felt sick. I thought that my opportunity to play in the NFL was over. Jules walked over to me and held me in her arms. She knew how much this meant to me.

Out of nowhere, my phone started ringing. It was a 313 area code. I picked it up, and it was a scout from the Detroit Lions.

He said, "Hey, Deon! I wanted to be the first to call you before any other teams reached out to you. We think you would be a great fit to battle for a spot on the roster and we would love for you to sign with the Detroit Lions."

I held the phone away from my mouth and screamed, "Let's go!" I dropped to my knees and started praying. I screamed, "Thank you, Jesus!" My phone started going crazy because the news got out fast that I had just signed with the Detroit Lions. Jules and I jumped around her apartment with so much joy.

It was one of the best times of my life. It was a dream come true. All that hard work had finally paid off. I called my grandma, screaming and crying.

"We did it, Granny! I just signed with the Lions! Let's go!" I felt my grandma's passion through the phone. She was super proud of me—not just for signing with the Detroit Lions—but for persevering through the struggle. After getting off the phone with my grandma, I talked with my agent. We both were super excited. This was a big deal for both of us. Alisa did everything I thought an agent would do. She sent a lot of emails, made a lot of phone calls, and advertised for me to different teams. Even though I signed with the Lions that year, it was still a roller coaster ride for me.

Football was going well, but my grandma was very ill around the same time training camp started. It was hard for me to focus because I knew she had little time left. I was going back and forth to the hospital and practice. My mind was everywhere. On top of that, I struggled with reading the playbook. The NFL playbook was much harder than the college playbook. On the first day of training camp, I walked right into our meeting room with a big surprise on my desk. It was the playbook. The playbook in college was a hard copy paperback. The NFL playbook was digital.

I flicked through the playbook and said to myself, "Not this again." At one of the proudest moments of my life, I was haunted by my reading problem. So many thoughts ran through my head at that moment.

"Deon, all you have to do is ask for help."

"Deon, don't you dare ask for help! Everybody is going to laugh at you!"

"Deon, why would you tell them you can't read? They are paying the best players millions of dollars to get the job done right, and you can't even read!"

"Deon, you asked for help so many times throughout your life. Nobody can help you learn how to read."

At that moment, I chose to stay quiet and suffer through the playbook.

Visiting my grandma at the hospital gave my brain a break from the playbook headache. I didn't want to worry my grandma with my problems, so I told her everything was going well in the NFL. I would sit on the side of the bed and tell her some stories about the superstars in the locker room. I told her how I sat next to Calvin Johnson, who was the Lions superstar wide receiver at that time. I was so nervous before practice started, so I busted out a quick rap flow to calm my nerves. Calvin Johnson was right next to me, bobbing his head and hyping me up as I rapped.

The whole team joined in. Afterward, we looked at each other and burst out laughing. I knew I couldn't rap, but I thought it was cool of Calvin Johnson to help me out as I built my confidence. My grandma knew my personality, so she thought that was the funniest story ever. When I used to leave the hospital, she was all I could think about. It was hard trying to change my mood. I remember being in the meeting room in a daze, thinking about when I was going to get that call from the hospital.

Instead of getting a call from the hospital, I got a call from the Detroit Lions front office.

Just like that, the Detroit Lions released me from the team.

Part of me was hurt. But again, I was very grateful for the opportunity. On the flip side of life, I was happy to spend more time with my grandma. I got a job with Starfish

Family Services, working with younger kids. I had such a great time with the little nuggets. Even though I struggled with reading, I used to enjoy reading to the little kids during nap time. I used to find the easiest book to read. That way, the kids wouldn't see me struggle. I got so good at avoiding reading throughout my life that I almost forgot that I couldn't read.

One day at work, my agent called and said she had some great news for me. "The Detroit Lions wanted to give you another shot at playing in the NFL!"

Once again, God gave me another chance at my dreams. The preseason had already started. The Lions had already played a few preseason games. Man, I was so happy to be back on the field. I told myself that I was going to stay focused, even with my grandma on my mind. We played the Jacksonville Jaguars. My tight ends coach looked me right in my face and said, "You're going to be playing this week, so you better be ready." I was excited.

I was on team three. I was in my zone, catching everything that came my way. I blocked until the play was over. I made a few mistakes, but I remembered what my old college coaches told me.

"If you're going to make a mistake, do it going fast."

That method worked. The coaches told me, "Great job, Deon! We love the effort, but wrong play or wrong block."

I even scored a touchdown running the wrong route. I made my way up the depth chart. Now, when practice was over, I had to face reality. I had to visit my grandma at the hospital. I could tell that her time was coming to an end because she couldn't really talk for an extended period of time.

I let my grandma know that my first game was coming up, and we were flying down to Florida. I told her I didn't know what to wear. I wanted to dress like I was this big-time superstar. She looked at me with a side face and said, "You better wear that blue suit that I bought you."

I wasn't tripping because I thought that blue suit was a banger. She also told me not to worry about her and to have a great time in Jacksonville. The next day, we loaded up everything and made our way to the airport. Jacksonville was very country and hot, but I had a great time. We ate at nice restaurants and traveled around with the team. That game was hype. We beat Jacksonville, and I got to play in the fourth quarter. This was a dream come true.

I made some really big plays in the game. After every practice or game, I was usually the last one in the locker room. I enjoyed having fun with the fans. I made it my duty to always give something away to the kids. I knew I was an inspiration to them. One day, my tight ends coach saw me showing love to the fans. As we walked into the meeting room, he said to the whole group, "We know who's happy to be on the team, and we know who wants to be on the team."

From his perspective, it looked like I was happy to be on the team because I showed love to the fans. However, he probably thought that I wasn't studying the playbook due to all the mistakes I made at practice. The NFL is a strict business.

Once again, the Detroit Lions released me.

I knew for a fact it wasn't because of my talent on the field. I truly believe it came from being tested on the playbook every day. I struggled so badly trying to understand the concepts and learn new plays. I was so scared to ask for help for many reasons. First, I didn't want to embarrass myself by telling grown men that I didn't know how to read. Second, the coaches deducted points every time we were late or missed an assignment. Lastly, I was tired of asking for help and *not* getting help.

After I was released from the team, my agent called again a few weeks later. The Detroit Lions were willing to give me another shot at making the team. I told my agent that I was walking away from football for good. Ms. Alisa thought I was crazy. She even mentioned other teams that were interested in signing me. She did everything she could to help me out. She even told me I should go overseas to play football. But I knew there would always be a playbook. I would always struggle to read the playbook. I had done everything I could to learn how to read, and I saw no point in reopening that wound when I couldn't fix it.

So, I walked away from football for good. A few days later, I went to visit my grandma at the hospital. She told me to do three things. First, she told me to move out of Detroit. She told me to go start a family of my own and to go forgive my mother. I heard the first two orders, but I didn't want to hear the last one. I actually thought my grandma was drugged up from all the medication. I said, "You want me to do what? Are you crazy? I already tried many times. I even moved her in with me during my time in college to help her with her drug problems. I tried over and over to help her, but she just kept disappointing me, and that hurt my feelings."

I said, "Granny, I love her so much. But I'm sorry. I can't."

My grandma looked at me with her big green eyes and gave me a "don't play with me" stare. Later that week, my grandma died at the hospital. We all gathered around her bed to say our goodbyes. I felt lost in the room. The person who knew me best was gone. Everything I did was to make her happy. There were other family members in the room. Some of them took advantage of her during her last years. I lost control of my emotions. It was my grandma's good spirit that kept me from beating them down. Once she passed away, I felt free to do whatever I wanted without feeling bad.

When the doctor pulled the plug, I blacked out, and my anger took over. That's when I charged at one of my family members, but my grandma's brother stepped in the way. Uncle Chuck was the person who saved the day. I don't remember much. But when he stepped in the way, I picked him up off the ground and had his feet dangling in the air. I posted his body against the hospital walls. That's when I realized the beast inside me had taken control. It wasn't until years later that I asked my uncle what happened that day.

Uncle Chuck told me, "Your grandma knew you were going to lose control and to make sure I looked after you when the time was right." My grandma was always a step ahead of me. She never stopped watching over me. That day in the hospital, I was full of rage and anger. After my grandma's funeral, I did exactly what I was told to do. I moved to Pittsburgh and started a new journey. Jules' family helped me pack and just like that, I was leaving Detroit.

God gives us tools in life so we can survive and develop a better version of ourselves. Anger is not one of those tools!

Running from the Truth

I thought moving to Pittsburgh was going to wash away all my pain and problems. I thought it would remove the pain from my childhood trauma, my pain from not knowing how to read, and my family problems. I wanted it to remove my pain from my grandma's death and my pain from being cut from the Detroit Lions. Instead of facing these issues, I chose to run from them.

When I moved to Pittsburgh, I stayed with Jules' parents. Honestly, I didn't want to. However, it was a great way to save money before we bought a house. Jules' mom and dad were very generous in allowing us to move in with them. There were rules and responsibilities I had to follow while I lived under their roof, but I expected that.

When I first moved in with the Makrinos family, the first thing we did was watch a movie called *My Big Fat Greek Wedding*. Jules' family is Greek. If you had ever seen that movie, you would have somewhat understood what Jules' family is like. In the Greek tradition, they do everything together. Making the adjustment to their lifestyle was difficult because my family did things very differently. I stayed in the basement while Jules slept in her room. The basement was like a house itself. It was pristine and had everything I needed. Every morning, Jules' dad or mom cooked breakfast for us, which was nice. I learned a lot from Jules' family over the years. Jules' dad owns his own business as a master plumber. So, some days, I worked side jobs with him.

In the meantime, my agent stayed in touch with me every other week. The NFL scouts reached out to her and thought that it would be a great idea if I went overseas to play football. They wanted me to get more experience. That wasn't a bad idea. Even though I struggled with reading the playbook, playing overseas football would've taken a lot of pressure off me. A few overseas teams were interested in my talent, including the CFL, China, and Australia. A low pay with a significant risk was still something I had to consider. I had some time to think it through. I also had to talk this over with Jules because she was a big part of my life. On the flip side of things, my family was still a problem. We never healed after my grandma's death.

My family members split up. Half of my family moved to Tennessee. The other half moved to Kentucky. Some moved around other parts of the Detroit area. Even though I lived in the suburbs of Pittsburgh, I still couldn't get as comfortable as I wanted. My family was always on my mind. My older brother was in prison, facing life. He didn't even get to say goodbye to my grandma. I can't even imagine how he felt. My other siblings called every day about a problem or something they needed. I felt like my grandma when she got stressed out. We were so used to my grandma fixing all our problems that we didn't know how to handle our own issues when she didn't. One day, I was lying down in the basement. I couldn't sleep.

I lay there, thinking about what my grandma told me to do. "Go forgive your mother." For a long time, I kept fighting it. I saw Jules' whole family eat at the dinner table. I wished my family had eaten dinner together. My mother was just getting out of rehab. During her time in rehab, she wrote letters to me and called me many times. I was too angry, stubborn, and upset to reply. She repeated the same mistakes. It was the same story, just a different day.

When I was a little boy, my mother would get drunk and beat me. She would get drunk and bug out on everybody. But, for some reason, she always came for me out of all her children. When I got older, I saw her for who she really was: evil and abusive. The pain always stayed with me. So, I stopped answering her calls and reading her letters.

When my grandma asked me to forgive her, that was a hard pill for me to swallow. Even though Jules' family was cool, I felt like I couldn't talk to them because they couldn't relate. No matter what, I had to obey my grandma's orders, whether I liked them or not. One night, I went out to my truck and called my mother. We talked for hours. At first, it was awkward and weird. But we decided to build a better relationship. My mother talked about how excited and proud she was of me. I told her the same thing. Even though we didn't talk every day, I did watch her progress.

I was happy for her and how her life was coming together. My mother told me she stopped using drugs and she wanted to be in her grandkids' lives. She kept asking me when Jules and I were going to have a baby.

I told her, "After we get married, as well as buy our first house."

We bonded that night on the phone. It was incredible. I heard my mother's happiness through the phone. We also talked about my older brother, Lawrence, who was in prison. This was a hard conversation for both of us. It felt unreal. My brother was an honor roll student. Prison and Lawrence in the same sentence never seemed to go together.

My mother started crying. She said, "I'm doing the best I can for him by writing him letters, sending him money, and keeping his spirits up."

That night, I asked her, "Can we start over and start spending time together?"

To be real, that was the best suggestion of the night. My mother said, "Of course, son." That year, I traveled to Tennessee a lot more and hung out with my side of the family. We all met at my mother's house to play card games and eat BBQ. It felt good being around my siblings again. I paid close attention to my mother because there was alcohol around. I wanted to see for myself if she was truly changed. My mother stood strong.

I watched my mother smile as she took mental pictures of her family having an amazing time. This was a fantastic feeling because she didn't need alcohol to enjoy the moment. That year, my mother and I became closer than ever. We talked a lot more, texted more, and planned more events.

I told my mother that Jules might be "the one." My mother has always approved of Jules since the first time they met when I was in college. I couldn't wait until I had my own place so my family could visit me. My truth was catching up with me. I needed to close the healing gap in my life, but I didn't know how. I'm happy that I listened to my grandma because I needed my mother in my life. I needed my whole family!

God was leading me to a higher version of myself. I needed to stop fighting with the truth and face it one day at a time. I didn't have the proper structure to form this beautiful picture, but I did have love. That's all I needed! When your intentions are good, God will help you as you build a foundation. That might be with your family, business, or personal goals. When you run from your problems, all you're doing is delaying the process. Take it one day at a time, and don't forget to give yourself credit. What I thought was pain turned out to be my peace!

Pay Attention to the Details

J ules and I bought our first house in 2016. However, the house needed a lot of work before we could move in. At first, I didn't approve of the house. From the outside, the house looked like junk. Jules' older brother Anthony didn't see junk. He saw a working project with a lot of potential. It was nice to have plumbers and carpenters in the family with a lot of experience. I didn't know much about fixing houses, but my work ethic was out of this world. I knew I would be able to fit right in with them as they worked on the house. When you are a good listener, you learn to blend in. We worked on the house as soon as we bought it. I stopped taking my medication after I graduated from college. Still, I knew I was going to need it if I wanted to stay focused during this time. We put hours into the house.

When Jules' dad gave me an assignment, I wouldn't take any breaks until the job was done. I worked day and night—literally. I didn't believe in taking lunch breaks or stopping. I enjoyed getting lost in my work. Jules and her family enjoyed lunch breaks because they loved spending time together as a family. There was nothing wrong with taking breaks. I just loved working and being in my zone. Breaks slowed me down or snapped my focus. Jules' dad would pull me aside and say, "It's okay to sometimes take a break and chat."

I told him how I liked to work, and he respected that about me. When everybody left, I'd stay and work extra hours because I felt good about the work I did. I wouldn't get back to Jules' family house until later, around 10:00 p.m. or even 11:00 p.m. It all depended on what I was working on. I loved doing demolition work, knocking down walls and ripping up the floors. Afterward, I would calmly clean up. Overall, we worked together as a team and finished rebuilding the house.

This project turned out perfect. It was like a brand-new house. It was a big accomplishment for us. But, really, this was a dream come true for me. I always lived in apartments or rented homes in the poverty-stricken community. To actually own a house in the suburbs and rebuild it was some next-level stuff for me. Jules and I settled into our new place, and things were going well for us. I was super thankful that Jules' family allowed me to stay with them. But it's nothing like having your own place and space.

Look at what God is doing for me. I worked so hard throughout my journey. Now, God blessed me to start a new chapter in my life with my girlfriend, dog, and a new house. I couldn't wait to tell my mother about the new house. I wanted to see the same happiness from my mother that I had seen when I had left college. I knew this was going to make my mother cry. I wanted her to see that I never gave up and that her son was still doing well.

I FaceTime'd my mother and showed her the whole house. Once she saw the house, she made plans to decorate and organize the house, just like a proud mother should. After a full year in our new house, Jules wanted to plan a vacation. She was going through a rough time. Jules' favorite auntie, Mrs. Dianna, passed away. It was just our luck that I had a few free vacation trips from the ESPYs. We had a free one-week trip to Esperanza, which was all-inclusive. This is an island located in Cabo San Lucas, Mexico.

A great idea popped into my head. *Maybe on this nice vacation, this would be the perfect time to ask Jules to marry me.* I planned the proposal in my head and how to organize it. I made a few calls to the resort so they could help me out.

Esperanza did an outstanding job bringing my vision to life. That week went perfectly. Jules didn't see it coming at all. I did a great job of disguising my plans for her. The whole time, I acted mad at her. I picked fights to see how she was going to react. Later that night, we had dinner by the ocean. The sky and moon were perfectly glooming.

However, I was anxious. There were so many people around, and I didn't know if she was going to turn me down or accept the proposal. The bartender was in on the surprise. He saw that I was sweating and had the jitters. He pulled me to the side and offered me a few drinks to cool down my nerves.

He gave me the best encouragement speech. I was grateful for him until I found out he charged me for those drinks. That night, I looked Jules in her eyes and thought to myself how lucky I was to have such a beautiful, intelligent person by my side. I asked Jules to stand up as I started to take a knee. She was literally freaking out before I could even bend down. Everybody turned to us as I reached one knee. I'm sure she didn't hear anything I said because she was stung with joy and excitement. As the night went on, everything moved in slow motion. I pulled out the ring, and I asked Jules if she would marry me. She said, "Yes!"

I was so nervous that I put the ring on the wrong finger, then I went in for a kiss. Everyone clapped and screamed with happiness. The Esperanza staff had perfect timing, from bringing out flowers, cake and ice cream to taking pictures. It was the best night ever. Jules called her mom, and I called my mom to share the good news. My mother was so happy for me that she started screaming through the phone. Honestly, it was the best feeling ever. My mother was so happy and excited that she started planning the wedding over the phone. I had to tell her to slow down. But I understand now she was happy to be involved.

Jules, on the other hand, was in her zone. She was busy showing off her ring and flossing around with a big smile on her face. We left the island the next morning and made it back home safely. At this point in my life, my dreams were coming together faster than I could blink. God granted me everything I asked for. All I had to do was meet Him in the middle and believe in Him.

Angry with God

My mother traveled to Pittsburgh a lot more. We built a stronger bond. I felt so comfortable and safe around her when she visited. She enjoyed the new house. My mother was amazed that I helped with the building process. I was excited to show her around the house. She knew this meant a lot to me because we never owned a nice house like this before. The times she visited me, she cooked, cleaned, and folded my laundry. I would play fight with my mother and tell her to just relax and allow me to take care of everything.

I wanted my mother to look at visiting me as a vacation. She always told me how stressful it was taking care of all her grandkids. My mother was trying to make up for the time with her kids. She overworked herself. So, when she came to visit me, I wanted her to enjoy her time with me peacefully. I wanted her to explore Pittsburgh without any problems. One afternoon, while I was frying chicken wings, my mother kept trying to help with the food. If you know me, you know I take pride in my cooking. When I cook, I cook to please my family and friends. My mother kept interrupting me. I had to give her that "Mama, I got this!" talk. She looked me in the eyes sternly.

"Deon, I just wanted to help. I want to do something for you that I'm good at. Something that will make me feel good about myself to be your mother."

How could I argue with that? After everything we've been through, I saw in her eyes that she wanted to be there for me. I saw it in her eyes that she truly loved me. I saw it in her eyes that she wanted me to forgive her. I told my mother she could help out just a little bit. I wanted her to try my amazing chicken without anybody's help. I wanted her to be proud of my cooking skills because I learned how to cook from her and my grandma. Even though they didn't teach me with instruction, I watched and learned from the best. After the food was done, we sat at the dinner table as a family. It was funny because my mother still tried to give me pointers after she ate the chicken to the bone. I had such a great time with my mother, but she couldn't stay for long.

Thanksgiving was approaching, and I thought it would be a good idea to ask the Makrinos family if my parents could join us for the first time at Thanksgiving.

Jules and I felt this would be perfect timing if we could all hang out and talk about wedding stuff at the table during Thanksgiving. Jules' parents thought that was a great idea.

They were excited to meet my parents for the first time. My mother and father were separated for a long time. This was going to be an epic moment for me.

Things were finally coming together, slowly but surely. Jules and I booked a bus ticket together for my mom and dad. My parents were going to leave on the 21st. After booking my mom's ticket, I called her. I was super excited to let her know that her bus ticket was all set. I'd already made plans to marinate the food so I could have everything tasting perfect. On November 18th, early Friday morning, my mother called me, and she sounded stressed out.

I asked her, "What's wrong?"

"Your brothers and sisters would be lost without me."

I didn't know what that meant. I figured it was because she had to watch the grandkids all the time.

I told my mother, "Hang in there! We're gonna have an amazing time at Thanksgiving."

I told my mother about all the wedding venues we had checked out. Jules and I didn't like any of them. But we had a good feeling about the one we were checking out on Sunday. Saturday, I went to work and had a fantastic time running a sports camp for the kids. I came home from work that day, excited about the wedding venue we were visiting the next day. But the next morning, I woke up with a bad feeling in my heart. I didn't know why, but something was wrong.

Jules' parents picked us up from our house to visit the wedding venue. An hour into the ride, my oldest sister called.

Jules looked at me and said, "Why is your sister calling me?"

I looked at her and said, "Because my mother just died."

Jules answered the phone, and she looked at me with unbelief. Jules hung up the phone and gave me the bad news. Jules' dad was driving at the time.

He asked, "Should we turn around?"

I said, "No. Let's still check out this venue." Honestly, I checked out. I remember driving to the venue, and the whole ride was super quiet. I couldn't believe it. I didn't want to believe it. We went to the venue and walked around. My phone was going crazy with calls from everybody. As we walked around, the tour lady was talking, but I couldn't hear anything. I told Jules and her family that I was headed to the car because I needed some time to myself. I sat in the car, thinking to myself, *This can't be true. Naw. God wouldn't do this to me right now.*

Everything was going perfectly. I was about to get married. I finally got my family together. I was living a great life. There's no way my mother was dead. My dad called me, but he had little words to say. He wasn't speaking or crying on the phone. We just sat there, breathing. That's how I knew it was true. He was at a loss for words. There wasn't much he could say to me. Jules' family took me back home.

I called my father and said, "I'm coming to pick you up, and we're going to Tennessee." I drove from Pittsburgh to Detroit to pick up my dad. He was at the casino, drunk. Then, I drove to Tennessee. The whole car ride, we said nothing to each other. I drove twelve hours, just lost for words. Once we arrived in Tennessee, I saw my siblings. They were hurt and crying with so much pain. It was hard to ask any question, but I did.

"How did she die? What happened? How are y'all? What do I need to do to help?"

I wanted answers, but I also wanted to support them. They told me my nephew found her in the hallway. She was unresponsive. My older sister told me that her son called her and told her that Granny was lying on the floor and she wasn't breathing. She told him to call the police.

When the police arrived, they did CPR and later pronounced her dead. The hospital refused to do an autopsy because she had been in the hospital a few times battling the flu. So, to this day, we still don't know how she passed away. My mother always battled with drugs. Honestly, my whole family battled with drugs. Half of my mother's brothers passed away from drugs. So, this could've been an overdose.

My mother's sister overdosed two weeks before in the same apartment, but she survived. I listened to my family argue about whose fault it was and what they wished they could've done. But it was too late to play the blame game.

We all took a role in helping with the funeral. My sisters were in charge of dressing my mother. I took care of the expenses and drove the kids back to Pittsburgh with me. My brothers were in charge of the flyers and everything else. When I made it back to Pittsburgh, I took the kids swimming and out to eat. My soul was broken. My heart was crumbled. As the kids were swimming, I sat there thinking to myself, *Where did I go wrong? My grandma just passed away. My brother is in prison for life. I just got cut from the Detroit Lions, and my mother just died.* I slowly felt myself losing control.

My mother's funeral was a complete blank for me. I remember bits and pieces. My friends and family talked to me, but I was in shock. There were people in my face, but I couldn't really hear what they were saying. Nothing made sense to me. I had just booked a ticket for her to visit me. I'd just talked to her. Now, she was dead and gone forever. After the funeral, I went back to Pittsburgh. I cried for days and nights. I cut my phone off and deleted my social media. In the blink of an eye, my world stopped!

The Deon everybody once knew had left the building.

Knock, Knock!

I slowly slipped into a depression, and I didn't even realize it. I'd never felt this before. My body was healthy, but my heart was broken. My spirit was weak. I went back to work a few weeks after my mother's funeral. I was a program director at the time, working with kids and youth. Things just didn't feel the same. I was drained. My coworkers checked up on me often. I was late to meetings, and I called off work. I couldn't hide the pain from my students. My true emotions always appeared.

When I was home, I kept to myself in the dark with the lights off and blinds closed. My life felt like it was falling apart. That's when Jules and I had the most problems. I needed someone to be by my side because I was in a battle. I expected Jules to help me through my pain. She wanted to, but she didn't know how. She was always at her parents' house at family gatherings. They were big on spending time together. I was battling something I couldn't control. I assumed Jules should've battled it with me. But she chose to spend time with her family instead.

Jules wouldn't get home until 10 p.m. nightly. When I wanted to talk or take my mind off the pain, she told me she was too tired, or she wasn't in the mood. Being in a bad mood all day can be contagious. I could see why she didn't want to be around me. We got into fights because I noticed more and more that I was spending time alone. As my future wife, I thought she was supposed to be there for me in times of need. But I spent many nights alone, battling depression. When I tried to talk to her, she told me I needed professional help. On one hand, she was right. On the other hand, I really needed somebody I could trust. When I saw that I couldn't talk to Jules, I hid my pain even more.

I went months without talking to my brothers and sisters. I didn't want them to see me this way. When we did talk, I told them I was doing well. But deep down, I was hurting. I was in so much pain that I couldn't express it with words.

Instead of giving my problems to God, I turned to drinking. One drink turned into a few drinks. Then, I started drinking every few days. After that, I drank every day and night. I drank 1800 tequila straight, no chaser. I drank the big bottle of Ciroc and Grey Goose. I hid the bottles in the upstairs attic so Jules couldn't find them.

I slowly lost control of my daily rituals. I prayed every night, but it wasn't sincere. I stopped working out and eating healthy. I bought shoes to cover up the pain. I wear a size 14½ so the shoes weren't cheap. When Jules questioned my spending habits, I gave her an excuse. The truth is I wanted attention from other people. That attention made me feel good about myself. Then, I started smoking marijuana. Smoking weed was the biggest game changer for me. See, I could only drink at night or when I got off work. I could never handle my liquor. I always got drunk and wanted to fight. The next day, I'd wake up with a hangover.

I managed to stay away from smoking marijuana for a long time. But when my mother passed away, I needed something to numb the pain. Smoking weed gave me what I was searching for. When Jules nagged about something, I was too high to even care. At work, I was able to tolerate the loud noise, and, most importantly, it kept me from feeling emotional about my mother's death. First, I started smoking to get through the day. Then, I started smoking to sleep. After that, I smoked my life away. I probably was smoking at least five to ten blunts a day. I learned that the drugs were just a temporary fix. My depression was getting stronger. I didn't care about anything in life.

I made new smoking friends. I did whatever I could to stay busy from thinking about the pain I carried. I stopped arguing my point of view with people, even when I knew the answer to the problem. I became a "Yes, sir!" man. I agreed with whatever people said. When I told Jules about my problems, she didn't pay any attention to me. So, I became friends with other girls who made time for me. When you're depressed with a broken heart, that's when you're the most vulnerable.

The pain in my heart grew colder. I had really long dreads, and I was stressed out to the point where I started losing my hair. I grew bald spots on top of my head. One day, I was at home playing Madden, which is a football game. Jules walked down the steps with a box full of empty bottles. She finally asked me.

"Are you okay?"

I looked at her and cried. I told her the truth about everything. I didn't care about life anymore. I told her I didn't care about her anymore. I told her I was depressed and I didn't know how to explain myself. I wanted to check myself into rehab or therapy. I needed to get better. I had to find that joy and happiness I once had in my life. I didn't have my grandma or mother to fix my problems this time. As a man, I needed to grow up and learn how to make better decisions. I needed to stop blaming everybody for my problems and take full accountability. It was me vs. me!

The first step was admitting that I had a problem. I needed professional help. Even though I didn't cause any problems to hurt anybody, my low energy still affected the people around me. The first mistake I made was not going to God. The second mistake I made was turning to drugs and alcohol. The third mistake I made was blaming Jules for not being there for me. I blamed anyone close to me.

Medications don't always taste good.

First Day of Therapy

For some reason, therapy has a bad reputation. The reason I know this is because I went to my first day of therapy with an attitude. Sitting in the waiting room, I thought to myself, *I don't need to be here. I don't have a problem. It's nothing wrong with me. What can a person do for me that I can't do for myself?* I didn't see it yet, but I was fighting my own healing journey. My first day was uncomfortable because I wasn't used to opening up to a stranger about my problems. So, of course, I only showed my therapist the good side of me. I already had it in my mind that there was nothing Mrs. Michelle could do to fix my problems.

I wasn't completely truthful about everything at the beginning of my therapy session. Mrs. Michelle asked me questions about my life, but I was short and gave her little details. I learned that you can never judge a book by its cover. After a few weeks in therapy, I let go of my ego. We got comfortable with each other. One day, she asked me a question that I couldn't answer right away.

She asked, "What do you like to do that makes you happy?"

"My grandma liked it when I played football."

"Well, that's nice. But what does Deon like to do?"

"My mother likes that I can cook and grill food really well."

"That's really nice. But again, what does *Deon* like to do?"

"Jules likes it when I'm being romantic and funny."

Mrs. Michelle, this time with a smile on her face, asked again. "What does *Deon* like to do to make *Deon* happy?"

This was a deep question. All my life, I trusted my grandma, and I wanted to make her happy. I found it easier to please others than myself. It made me feel good to see other people happy, even if it cost me my happiness.

Mrs. Michelle said, "Well, I want you to find out what makes Deon happy in this world."

She gave me a few tips and strategies. One tip she gave me was the concept called R.A.I.N. It stood for Recognize, Accept, Investigate and Nurture. She explained to me what they meant, and she wanted me to apply it to my life.

In 2018, I started going back to the gym and exercising a lot more. One day, I woke up, and I said to myself, "I'm going to start running." I hated running unless it was for a sport like basketball or football. Mentally, running was going to be a challenge for me. I went to the trails and ran four miles. It was draining. Those four miles were the hardest thing I did that year. But it felt good. One mile turned into two miles. Two miles turned into three miles. Before I knew it, I'd run four miles. Once I learned how to be consistent, I saw improvement. I lost a lot of weight quickly, and I was fit.

I felt good about myself. In 2018, I started checking in and checking out. I daydreamed throughout the day; I was going through a hard time. I was fighting myself, trying to hide my pain. Instead of facing my reality, I tried to sweep my problems under the rug. My homeboy L.T., who I played football with in college, was drafted by the Steelers. It was a blessing to have someone I knew from Michigan in Pittsburgh. L.T. knew what I was going through when it came down to my mother's death. I was able to escape reality when I spent time around him and his family. It was nice to be able to go to some of the Steelers games for free. I was living my dream through him. We both looked out for one another. I took care of his dogs and his house while he was either at practice or traveling. L.T. is a big family person, and we both knew the importance of keeping a house together.

He has the coolest mother ever. Her name is Ms. Sandra. She has always treated me like her other son. She told us when we were right and when we were wrong. When I went home, I had to face reality again. Some days, the pain would get too heavy. That's when I started drinking again. Even when I told myself I was going to quit, I found an excuse for why I needed just one more sip. I learned that when you're in the healing process, it's going to take time. I'm talking about months, years, or even more.

I was struggling to accept my mother's death. I also was struggling with finding true happiness and joy. If I truly wanted to heal, I needed to learn how to accept the things that happened in life. I practiced the R.A.I.N. concepts, but that didn't work right away. When I felt pain, I looked for a quick fix. I looked for something to make me feel good right away. But that was the problem. I wasn't sure what helped me or hurt me. I went days without sleep. I picked up smoking again to calm me down. That's when I learned something new about myself: I have an addictive personality.

There are good addictions and bad addictions. I couldn't tell them apart. I told my therapist the weed helped me, and she approved of it. So, I monitored myself, keeping a schedule of my moods. As 2018 was coming to an end, I learned I was going to have to face my problems, no matter if I liked it or not. I also needed to forgive others—not for them—but for myself.

Therapy helped. I saw improvement, but some things just don't happen overnight.

Letting Go of Toxic People

In 2019, I had to relearn myself. My face showed when I was stressed out and when I was doing well. I learned how to put myself first. I took control of my life. But first, I needed to find out the cause of my stress. That's when I saw the biggest problems within the people around me. When other people learn how to stress you out, they use that to their advantage. I prayed to God that He would help me reveal the people in my blind spots. So, I started with my family.

My older brother was a blind spot. Whenever he called me, he called for favors or to complain about something. Lawrence never accepted his responsibility. He blamed his prison situation on our childhood. He often said we never got a fair shot in life because of our parents. He pointed the finger at everybody but himself. He spent our whole phone conversation talking about other people and their problems. He never once asked me how I was doing. When I didn't do something for him, he snapped at me or used his story to weaken me to feel sorry for him. He manipulated me. He knew I would do anything for him, so he took advantage of me.

Lawrence always called me lucky. He said I cheated my way through college. He bashed me and guilt-tripped me. He never gave me my true respect.

After all I did for him, he truly never appreciated my time and effort. He even got so low as to blame my mother's death on me. Prison turned my brother into a monster, or prison showed me his *true* identity. One day, I got so tired of the bull crap that I snapped on him. I called him out on everything. We got into a huge argument. That's when I realized I needed space. Once I stopped answering his calls, I watched him turn my family against me. It hurt my soul to see my little brothers pick his side. I didn't realize how much power Lawrence had over us. My older brother was toxic, and he had to go until he fixed his ways!

I got a new job working as an educational liaison, helping foster kids get into college and helping them in their personal lives. Being an educational liaison brought me so much joy. So, I was able to distract myself from the people I'd cut out of my life. I knew my siblings were hurting like I was hurting from my mom's death. So, I gave them their space. One thing my older brother was right about is the fact that our father's absence played a big role in our lives. My grandma and my father didn't get along when I was a child.

My grandma told him the truth about himself, and my daddy didn't like that. My daddy never kept his promises. He was an alcoholic, and he had a gambling problem.

When we were younger, he promised he would take us to the game. My brothers and I would stay up all night waiting for him. Later that night, my brothers lost hope. They knew he wasn't coming to pick us up. But I was the one who kept the faith. I stayed up all night with my bags packed, staring out the window. He never showed up. My grandma didn't play any games when it came down to doing the right thing. She was the one who had to pick up our hearts and glue them back together when he didn't show up. We wouldn't see our father for weeks. When we did see him, we still loved him the same. On the days that my dad did keep his promises, he would sit outside in the car because he was scared of my granny. My daddy was another blind spot. I tried pleasing him so he would notice me. But he kept running from me. I didn't know why.

Instead of cutting my daddy off, I chose to build a stronger relationship with him. My father had already missed half of my life. I didn't want him to miss the other half. I wanted him to know that when times got hard or challenging, I was the one who stood strong. The Word of God says we must honor our mother and father. My daddy was the only parent

I had left. So, I didn't mind going back to Detroit and going fishing with him just to spend quality time with him.

My father experienced a lot of trauma when he was growing up. Because he had to grow up really fast, he dropped out of high school and entered the car industry. My father only had an eighth-grade education. I felt like it was the perfect time for us to break the generational curse. So, we learned to forgive and love one another. My high school friends were also blind spots. When I went back to Detroit to visit, I always saw high school friends. That's when I learned some people don't want to change. They are satisfied with their current lifestyle. I also learned that you are who you hang around. The things my friends did didn't line up with my highest self.

I'm not perfect, but I wanted to get better. If that meant cutting off my arm to save the rest of my body, so be it. This season of my life was hard. I broke away from things that made me comfortable. I learned how to be uncomfortable. I had to allow God to remove the people who weren't causing me any good in my life so He could make room for the people who would help me grow. But first, I needed to learn how to be on my own. Jules and her family were also a blind spot. Since the first day we moved to Pittsburgh, I felt like Jules overlooked me. My voice didn't count like everybody else in her family. I'm not saying I didn't matter, but no one took me seriously.

Jules and I needed to separate ourselves from everybody else. I needed her to put me first in our relationship since we were about to get married. This was tremendously difficult for Jules to understand. Her family came first in her eyes. Jules argued with me. She couldn't see the full picture. I already knew this was going to take some time, so I decided to work on myself instead of forcing her to see my point of view.

During my time alone, I learned I was sleepwalking. I got up in the middle of the night just to eat junk food. I also researched and found that this could be a symptom of stress. I did everything I could to eliminate the causes of my stress. I was tired of hiding that I had a bald spot on top of my head. I was so ashamed that I started buying hats or covering it up with hair spray. That's when I decided to cut my dreadlocks. I saw no point in holding on to something that was stressed out. It was time for a new look. I was building a new me. I had my dreads for years, and I loved my hair. But stress and my toxic ways had to go.

Goodbye, dread-headed Deon!

Faith Can Heal Wounds

My wedding date was in three months. I couldn't picture myself getting married without my mother by my side. I needed to find a way to let go of the past and make this about Jules and me. Genesis 2:24 says, *Therefore a man shall leave his father and his mother and hold fast to his wife, and they shall become one flesh.* I was so close to completing all my dreams and goals. Kavon Frazier, who played safety for the Dallas Cowboys, invited us to his wedding. We played football together in college and built a strong relationship over the years. Jules and I loved Kavon and his wife Gera's wedding. It was so romantic!

I'll never forget when Kavon and his mother went out on the dance floor. Kavon's mother battles with Amyotrophic Lateral Sclerosis (ALS). The disease caused her to be paralyzed from the waist down. But to see them on the dance floor together was beautiful. As they danced, I was daydreaming that it was me out there dancing with my mother. Tears fell because I saw the way Kavon looked at his mother. He had so much joy in his eyes. I met

Kavon's mother in college, and she has one of the most beautiful hearts.

When Kavon was on his recruiting visit to college, I was his host. I told his mother I was going to always look after Kavon, and that's what I did. We became football brothers, and Kavon's mother respected me for that. Watching Gera and Kavon get married brought Jules and me together even more. Their wedding gave us great ideas. I spent a lot of time with my siblings leading up to the wedding. I realized we were all battling my mother's death in different ways. In order for us to reunite, we needed faith. Losing a loved one can cause a lot of damage to the heart, but having faith can heal wounds. I couldn't just start something and not finish it. I needed my family.

I was so appreciative of Jules' family for help in preparing for our wedding. It also felt good to see my family working as a team. To see both of our families work together meant so much to me and Jules. We had a cookout the day before the wedding. Even though I couldn't picture myself without my mother at my wedding, I was able to picture myself with the rest of my family. I watched my dad, uncles, brothers, and sisters having a great time. This is what my grandma meant when she said, "God and family are priceless." Having faith is what brought my family back together.

My Wedding Day

Dreams really do come true. Since I was a little boy, I always pictured myself getting married and having a family. Our special day had finally arrived. My life was about to change forever. Nobody can prepare you for the emotions that come with getting married. I'm thankful for my family and friends like Jason, L.T., Kavon, my godfather Pate, my uncle Patrick, and many more who supported me. I was extremely nervous in the dressing room. It felt like I was getting ready for a football game. The music played while we got amped up.

Jason, who was my Best Man, played a critical role. I needed him to make sure that I didn't get cold feet. He had to keep me calm. He was already a year into his marriage, so he truly understood what I was feeling.

My little brother Demarco, who was also one of my groomsmen, walked up to me and said, "I'm so proud of you. Thanks for leading the way in this family." That meant a lot to me because that's all I was trying to do. I just wanted to be a great leader in my family. Before the wedding started, my daddy walked up to me. I finally saw a tear drop from his eyes.

He gave me a strong hug and said, "I love you, son, and I'm proud of you!" I cried because that was my first time hearing my dad say, "I love you."

My dad comes from a family where men don't express themselves with words like, "I love you," and they don't give hugs. So, when my dad said those magical words, that's how I knew God was with us. I also felt my mother's spirit when my dad and I were bonding. I felt joy, happiness, and peace. As I walked outside, I noticed that the weather was perfect. It was sunny and slightly cloudy. It wasn't too hot, but not too humid. It was a beautiful scenery. The view was amazing. As I looked around, I embraced the moment. I saw people taking their seats with little kids running around having fun. Most importantly, I saw my family, coaches, and mentors smiling at me with happiness.

When the music started playing, my heart slowed down. First, the flower girls walked down the aisle. They were so beautiful. It was nice to see my niece be a flower girl. I knew that it meant a lot to my older sister, Nancy, to see her daughter be a part of something so special. Then, the bride's music started playing. Everybody stood up from their seats.

I saw this beautiful girl come out in this gorgeous dress. It was all white and very luscious, like a sweet taste of wine.

Jules looked amazing. I did my best not to let a tear drop from my eyes, but I couldn't fight it. I was at my all-time happiness. It's a feeling you just can't put into words. When a person is truly happy for you, it shows in their character. I looked at my groomsmen and saw my little brother with tears in his eyes. My little brother Marco had one foot in the streets and one foot in becoming a great mentor. His emotions showed me he was genuinely happy for me. When Jules and I finally reached each other, it was like the stars reaching the sky. We said our vows to each other and held hands. I couldn't wait to kiss her and make her Mrs. Butler. I was officially married. Now, it was time to party and have a great time.

The groomsmen and bridesmaids walked out to nice music and good old-fashioned dancing. It was the funniest thing in the world because people had the chance to show off their dance moves. It was new school vs. old school. My daddy showed off those old Temptations moves. Everybody had a great time. The crowd was diverse, with Blacks, Whites, Greeks, and Mexicans. Then the deejay called for the daddy/ daughter dance. Watching Jules and her dad dance was priceless.

Mr. Makrinos did an outstanding job raising his daughter. These are moments a father will never forget. When it was my turn to come out with my mother, because my mother was deceased, I chose to come out with my older sister Makieda. Makieda and I always had different views of life. This caused us to have resentment toward one another. We both needed to learn how to come together and get along. This was the perfect time to connect with each other by slow dancing and absorbing each other's energy. I needed my big sister, but I didn't know how to communicate that to her with words. We held each other tight and rocked back and forth to the song "Mama" by Boyz 2 Men.

We both cried. Then, I put my head on her shoulder, drowning myself with tears. The rest of my brothers and sister stood up and made their way to the dance floor. We all hugged each other in one big group. The pain was real. It was hard for people not to cry. You couldn't tell me that my mother's spirit wasn't in the room because Makieda pulled us all back together as we were soaking in grief. We wiped the tears from our faces and started smiling. We all knew she wasn't too far from us.

In that moment, we changed history. Instead of pushing each other away, we allowed ourselves to slowly heal as a family. That's when the deejay called both sides of the families to the dance floor. But it was the little kids who stole the show of the night. They were out there on the dance floor with the new generation's dance moves. I'm truly blessed that God pulled me back together so I could enjoy this wonderful time. God's timing is perfect! After everything was over, around 11 p.m., Jules and I had to drive to the hotel and then to the airport at 4 a.m. to catch our flight for our honeymoon.

We were headed on a Royal Caribbean cruise, which stopped at seven different islands. That was my first time on a cruise ship. I highly recommend it to anybody who has never been on a cruise. We had the best time of our life. Yes, we both got motion sickness. But after a day or two, we were okay. It had multiple casinos, all-inclusive food, basketball courts, movie theaters, and so much more. When we stopped on the islands, we explored and had a lot of adventures. When the trip was over, I could say it was truly worth it. We made it back safe and sound. Now that we were married, the next step was starting a family. However, I needed to keep up with my health plans and continue doing the things that made me a stronger man.

Dark vs. Light

Once we got back from our cruise, it was like traveling from another portal. We were gone for a week, which was a long time for me. I was so happy to see my dog Ace and the rest of my family. My dad and Uncle Topcat watched the house while we were on vacation. Jules and I came back home to so many wedding gifts and pictures. I needed the pictures because everything was happening so fast at our wedding that I couldn't capture every moment. As we settled back into our normal lives, I wanted to visit my family and friends who couldn't make it to the wedding. As soon as I arrived in Detroit, the first person I called was my big cousin, Mo.

Even though we both took different paths in life, I never judged him. I always showed him respect. My cousin Mo is a real street gangster, but I still loved him because we are family. We drove right to the barbershop, which is called 6 a.m. I knew the owner, as well as everybody who was there for a haircut. I was with the fellas, laughing and cracking jokes. This was the beginning of the setup. I let my guard down whenever I got around Mo. He was the only one who truly knew our deep family business when it came down to my brother Lawrence and my cousin Whop. We were sad that it broke up our family.

Mo talked about how somebody owed my cousin Whop some money. I told him whoever it was needed to pay that man his money because I knew Whop didn't play any games. As Mo talked, I listened and paid close attention to what he said. What I didn't know was that Mo was just feeding me to the sharks. As soon as I made it home, I reached out to my cousin Whop to let him know the bad news. Reaching out to Whop and acting as a messenger was probably one of my biggest mistakes. My whole purpose was to stay away from drama.

On the other hand, I was so happy to see my wife when I made it back to Pittsburgh. I felt good calling Jules my wife. We both sat down and talked about how busy we were with working. We thought it would be a great idea if we got another dog so Ace wouldn't be home alone while we were at work. We picked up another pit bull and named her Uno. We laughed so hard once we walked into the house with Uno in our hands because of Ace's facial expression. Dogs have emotions, as well. We had a happy family. The only thing we were missing was a little Butler running around the house. Having a child was the next step I was looking forward to, but we first needed to enjoy our marriage!

My cousin Whop contacted me and we talked on JPay. JPay is a way for inmates to text their loved ones and receive funds. I hadn't spoken to Whop in years. So, I was trying to update him on everything. He seemed happy for me, but I was also sad because I knew he didn't have any good news to share with me. Prison is a step closer to hell. As we talked, I told him how I wanted to get our families back together. Their prison situation broke up the family even more.

When Whop wrote to me, something weird happened. It's like his energy was traveling with his words. I felt his emotions. I heard his voice in my head as I read his letters. So, we started writing to each other every day. I felt like he was trapping me, but I didn't understand how. When we talked about Lawrence, I told him Lawrence was still the same, manipulating and controlling. But Whop was doing the same thing. I walked right into a trap. They heard about all the great things I was doing in the world. They heard about how I was walking in the light and bringing joy to those stuck in darkness. Whop thought he could use the power of fear to run me away. This broke my heart even more.

I thought families were supposed to love each other. I thought families were supposed to be there in times of need. But some family members are there to cause you to stumble. One day, as I was writing, I felt a big energy wave jump on me. This energy was powerful. It felt cold and dark. I was dizzy. That's when I bent down to my knees and prayed to God, asking Him to protect me.

Before I could fully move forward in my life, I needed to go backward and heal from my past trauma. That's why I'm writing this book. I didn't know Satan's dark secrets, but I wasn't about to allow him to take over my life. I realized every family has at least one or two demons in their bloodline, but God gives us free will. God gives us a choice to make. We can follow the light or walk in the dark. I chose to walk in the light!

Enlightenment is a gift from God.

School Teachers Only See Half the Story

I wanted to forget about everything I'd been through and start fresh. But in reality, life just doesn't work that way. It was the start of a new year, 2020, to be exact. I didn't know it yet, but my world was about to change again. I have so much passion for helping youth. As an educational liaison, a lot of the kids on my caseload were either in foster care or homeless. I had a few kids who were in the correctional facility. But no matter what, I didn't judge because I knew what it was like growing up in the system. I knew what it was like not having a meal to eat or not having the best family support.

So, every day that I went to work, I wanted to give my all to each student. I started off with sixty kids on my caseload. That was a lot, but I didn't complain because I felt like a superhero to them. They loved me, and I loved them. As an educational liaison, my job responsibilities were to help kids with their school work, grades, college applications, and financial aid. I did home visits. Even though their homes weren't safe all the time, I still felt comfortable. My mission and my goals were more significant. Supporting these youth and giving them a better opportunity was my main objective. I went above and beyond for them, coming out of my own pocket to make sure they had food to eat.

I visited the students at school, taking them on college tours or dropping them off at work. Even though I couldn't spell that great, I always found a way to get the job done. When it was time to turn in our weekly reports, I made sure I went the extra mile to use Google or spell check. I also asked a co-worker or someone else to look over my work before I turned it in. Some days, I attended IEP (Individualized Education Plan) meetings. I also went to court hearings for the teens on my caseload. In those meetings, I was reminded of my childhood, causing me to be in my feelings. That's why I didn't mind going all out for the kids on my caseload. I was inside looking in. I knew what it was like to struggle with schoolwork and to be hungry at the same time. One day, as I was headed to an IEP meeting, I was with one of my youths. We had a heart-to-heart conversation.

I asked him, "What's the problem with your grades? And why are you acting out in school?"

He let down his ego and told me the truth during that car ride. He told me he was having a hard time in school. He said, " I don't feel like I'm smart enough for school."

I thought if I told him my story of struggling in school, how I couldn't read, and how I grew up in the ghetto, it would help him believe in himself more. Unfortunately, after I told him my story, he didn't even believe me because I was so professional at my job.

I told him during the car ride, "Sometimes you just have to tell the teacher you need extra help. That's what I did in college. I asked for extra help."

Once we got into the IEP meeting, the other school workers were down his back, giving him a hard time. The teachers only reported bad things. I watched this kid put on a gangster's face and act like he didn't care. It hurt my feelings because I saw myself in this kid. I knew what he felt. I knew the shame of not feeling smart enough for the school system. The way the teacher put him down in front of all the other workers only made matters worse. The teacher showed us his schoolwork, and it reminded me of my handwriting, spelling, and grammar. I thought to myself, *Maybe it's not the student. Maybe it's the teacher or the system!* This kid was already in foster care. He'd had three different caregivers in the last year. He didn't play any sports or have anybody pushing him. So, of course, he was going to slip right through the system.

I was blessed to play sports and have a great support system. But there were so many kids on my caseload who had some of the same similarities as this young man. As much as I tried to be Superman, I'm only Deon. After a few months of working my tail off, I watched my caseload grow from sixty to 105. I was stressed out and frustrated. I asked my supervisor if I could close out some of my kids on my caseload.

He said, "No, due to the rules. Also, some kids might come back to the program."

I didn't like that answer, but I did respect it. I was burned out and underpaid for the work I did. Being on Adderall helped me focus and get my work done, but of course, Adderall has side effects. So, I had to work extra hard to complete my job duties in a certain time frame. I tried my best never to take work home with me. I learned to keep a work/life balance from my days in sports. But it was impossible due to so many kids on my caseload. Months went by, and I grew more frustrated with my job because they made new rules every other week, giving us more than we could handle.

A lot of the caseworkers quit, so we had to take on their responsibility. I felt like I was drowning in work. When you can't spell or read very well, life is difficult. I doubted myself again, burning myself out just to write an email. I went from being a superhero to wanting to be a villain! My monthly review was coming up after my meeting was over.

I felt like maybe it was time to pick a different career path. My supervisor said my work ethic was amazing, and my performance was excellent. But, I needed to improve on writing summaries and reviews about what I did for a student. I wasn't able to get the raise I deserved. I can't lie. That crushed my spirit.

I started to lose hope because I didn't know how to express my work on paper. Slowly, I started making my way back to the streets. That's when I got the idea to start selling weed so I could make some extra money. Then, I started making money fast. I didn't have to write any reports or send any emails about it. I was tired of giving my all and still coming up short to something I had no control over. On one hand, I can see why kids who struggle in school give up. The system is not built for them to win.

On the other hand, we need an education to be successful in this world. Then, "Boom!" That's when the world walked right into a pandemic. I saw everything that I was sweeping under the rug and more. All my life, people have told me to keep going and never look back. But then, the world basically stopped due to the coronavirus. That's when I was forced to see my truth within this world.

Teachers, we need you more than we think!

Running Into My Truth

During the pandemic, I had a hard time. My schedule was off. Everything was closed down. I couldn't go to the gym, so I built one in my basement. I spent a lot of time in the house. That's when I noticed that I was a busybody. I couldn't sit still. I was cooking, cleaning, working out, and playing video games. I tried to stay busy so I wouldn't think about my mother or my past. I was running out of things to do, and that's when I decided to go for a run to see if I could clear my head. I ran four miles, and it felt good. I was able to distract myself from all my problems. The next day, I ran another four miles, and that felt even better. I ran four miles consistently every day for at least two weeks.

During one of my runs, I said to myself, *I'm just going to keep running.* I wanted to challenge myself. The breeze on my runs felt great. I noticed how beautiful the trees were. I heard the birds chirping. I watched people smile as I ran past them. It felt good to get lost in the moment. Then I heard in my running app, "You just reached ten miles." I said, "Wow!

I can't believe that I just ran ten miles without feeling any pain." So, I set a goal to one day run twenty miles.

During one of my runs, I attempted the twenty miles without any training. I reached 14.45 miles. That's when my body shut down. I was sick to my stomach I didn't reach my goal. I had to walk back to where I started. I was in so much pain that I felt like my hamstring was on the floor, and I was dragging it. My body was aching. I felt dehydrated. I motivated myself to finish my walk as I dragged my legs. I was at least six miles away from my truck. I wasn't in any condition to make it back home by walking. It took everything inside of me to call my father-in-law. After he picked me up, it was an emotional rollercoaster ride back home. I snapped at him, screaming and yelling at him. I cried because I didn't finish what I started. Mr. Makrinos was calm as he asked me if I'd ever run twenty miles before?

I answered him with so much passion. I screamed at him, saying, "No! But tomorrow, I am going to try again and best believe that I'm going to reach my goals." I couldn't figure out why I was taking my anger out on him. Mr. Makrinos was respectful and understanding. He allowed me my moment of frustration. He was calm that whole car ride. The next day, I woke up early. I was determined to reach that twenty miles. Long story short, I failed at ten miles.

As I walked back, I had my head up high. I started having a conversation with myself. I asked myself, "Why did I attempt to run twenty miles with no experience? Why am I so angry?" I laughed because a part of me knew the truth. So, I made a promise to myself to start training by setting small goals. I also needed to do some research before I could run the big twenty miles. Every day that I woke up, I ran. But, this time, I had a purpose. That's when I started having a conversation with God. It was a conversation that needed to happen. I had a bunch of questions to ask Him. I wanted to focus on the main one, which was my mother's death. I needed to find peace with myself. I needed answers!

I asked God, "Why did you take my mother away from me? We were in the middle of building a stronger relationship. Things were finally coming together between us. I did everything that I was supposed to do. My mother was getting her life together, and we were working hard to build a better family. Then You took her from me!"

I ran harder. I know this might sound strange to most people or even like blaspheme in a case. But that's when I heard God's voice say, "Why don't you just ask her yourself?"

As I ran, I heard my mother's voice. She said, "Deon, I'm so proud of you!"

I said, "Wait a minute! Ma, is that you?"

She responded, "Yes!"

For a minute, I was shocked to hear her voice. Deep down, I was super excited. I was thankful that God allowed me to talk with my mother. I conversed with her as I ran.

"Ma, I have something to ask you?"

She said, "Sure. Ask me anything. But just know that I'm cheering for you."

"Ma, why did you treat me that way when I was a kid? Why did you hate me so much?"

"I didn't hate you. I was hurting myself. I didn't mean to hurt you. I started drinking and blacking out!"

"But Ma, why did you take it out on me?"

"Because I saw myself in you, the love, the passion, and the joy. I didn't know how to communicate with you. So when I hit you and gave you whoopings, I'd hit you harder. When I saw that you could take it, I thought it would make you stronger."

"Ma, I'll talk to you later!" I had just reached my weekly goal during my run. I looked forward to my runs and being able to talk with my mother. So I ran with more joy in my heart. During some of my runs, my mother popped up on me and said, "Go, Deon! You the man! You can do it! You got this." One morning, I heard, "Hi, son. Are there any more questions today?"

"Yeah. Why didn't you come to more of my football games in college?"

"Do you remember when I came to live with you while you were living in your apartment at school?"

"Yeah."

"Well, I was embarrassed. I said to myself, my son is taking care of me while he's in college. After all I put him through, and he still loves me. My son wanted to see his mother doing well. I was also exposed to a life that I never saw before. I had so much fun with you. I saw that you were happy and I didn't want to mess that up for you. Deon, you encouraged me to get my life together, and I loved you so much for that. I enjoyed every minute of college with you. I'm sorry I missed your games. I wish things could have gone differently."

"Wow! I didn't know you felt that way, Ma." I started crying and running harder. My emotions got the best of me. So, I said, "Ma, I have to go. I'll talk to you tomorrow." When I wasn't running or working out, I practiced putting myself first. I worked on the things my therapist taught me. I found out more about myself and the things that made me happy. Jules and I talked more and worked on our relationship. I felt good about myself and the changes I made in life. I ran every day, confessing my sins and fasting!

During one of my difficult runs, I encountered a hill. I struggled running up this hill to get to the other side. As I ran up the hill, my thoughts kicked in, telling me I couldn't do it! For a minute, I believed them. I heard my mother's voice saying, "Deon, you got this! You can do it, baby. Believe in yourself! I believe in you, son. Dig deep down, and don't you dare give up! You bet not stop. You're almost there. Let's go! You can do this! Deon, tell yourself you got this."

I told myself, "I got this! I can do it." Before I knew it, I was over the hill. I said, "Thank You, God, and thank you, Ma! I truly needed that."

My mother said, "Deon, no matter what, I will always be with you!" After my runs, I recognized something new.

I learned that I was spiritually gifted. I also gained my confidence back. I realized that I was on a journey to greatness. For the longest, I was looking at my mother's death all wrong. God didn't take my mother away from me. He gave me an extra year before she died to build a better relationship with her. God spoke through my grandma as she was passing away when she told me to go forgive my mother. I didn't know it then. But now, it all makes sense. Once I accepted my truth, I started seeing better.

Even though people died in the pandemic, I felt like I was waking up. I felt good about who I was becoming and where I was going in life. Healing is truly a process. I'm blessed for every minute, every hour, and every day that God gives me.

You know that you're healing when your thoughts are healthier.

Discovering Dyslexia

During the pandemic, many people got sick and died. People were dropping like flies; the death rate was at an all-time high. One article reported that over three million people died due to COVID-19. The government mandated everybody to work from home. After a few months had passed, my job started laying people off because we didn't have to go to work, schools, or homes. The Educational Liaison Department was the only role in the safe zone. But we still had to work extremely hard because we had a lot of seniors going off to college.

Working from home caused a lot of frustration for me because of my reading and spelling issues. We had to make sure all our kids did their online work. The students needed help with writing papers and understanding their school assignments. I couldn't help them in the way I would have liked to help. I felt like I was failing at my job. I even felt like I was going backward after turning to the streets to sell drugs. So, I started smoking weed again to escape my reality. I had problems that I couldn't figure out.

My supervisor mentioned they might be firing people from our team. I thought I might be the first to go. In the meantime, Jules and I got to spend a lot of time together at home. We worked out together, went for walks, and watched TV shows. We talked about a time when we should plan for a small family of our own. Jules read in a book that it normally takes at least five to six months for a woman to get pregnant after coming off birth control. But I told her that it was only going to take us a month because my soldiers marched strong. She laughed and said, "Scientifically, that's impossible because I've been on birth control for years."

The next month, I was drained from work. I was burned out. As one of my work days came to an end, Jules came over and asked if we could talk. She was acting weird. She was extremely careful with her words. She reached behind her back and pulled out a baby tee shirt. Jules was pregnant. I went nuts. I almost passed out. We both were excited. I screamed and said, "I told you God was going to bless us! I knew it!"

After I calmed myself down, we both agreed not to tell anybody until the time was right. I woke up the following day and went for my daily run.

Deep down, I was freaking out about becoming a father. However, I was also super excited. I wanted to tell the world. But first, I needed to talk with God. During my run, I started to repent again, telling the truth. I told God that I couldn't read well and that I was embarrassed about the way I learned. I told God I wanted to be able to read to my child. But I didn't know why I couldn't read at a high level. I worked really hard, and I tried my best with literature. But I couldn't see the words or pronounce them the right way. As I ran, I started crying because I thought about my childhood. I thought about how people picked on me for not knowing how to read. I didn't want my child to know that I struggled with reading. After I got done repenting, I heard God say, "Go fight for education! Go tell the world your story."

"How can I fight for education when I don't even know how to read or spell?"

"I will be with You during your journey. I'll tell You how and what to say."

I respect God, and I have faith in Him. So, I didn't hesitate. I asked if I could talk with my mother and grandma. I couldn't wait to tell them the good news. This was the best feeling ever. In my heart, I know they were so proud of me. After my run, I decided to buckle down and own up to my education.

I went on Amazon and bought a bunch of books to help with my reading problem. I bought *Basic English Grammar for Dummies and English Grammar: 100 Tragically Common Mistakes (and How to Correct Them)*. I promised myself that I was going to learn how to read to my child. So, I started studying hard, day and night. I had to figure out how to become a better reader. As I taught myself, I noticed a few things I had problems with while trying to read. One, I skipped words and looked right past a word. When I read a sentence, I noticed that I was skipping words like "the, is, was, a, and I." I couldn't pronounce the smallest words, which was frustrating for me. But I kept practicing. Two, I got headaches. The more I stared at a word, the stronger my headaches got. Three, I felt like my brain was playing mind games with me because the words moved around. I needed to learn how to take breaks.

As the world got darker during the pandemic, I saw things a bit clearer. Once the lights went out in the world, the rats and roaches came out. Then, I saw people come after me. But I didn't know why.

I did what God told me to do. I posted about my struggles with education on my Facebook page. That's when my problem became bigger. Some people in this world are not a fan of God or the light. When I say people came after me, I mean my closest friends and family members. I lost friends who I thought had my back, but it turned out to be different. I felt like they wanted me to pick the dark side or stay in sin. If you can't tell yet, I have a very aggressive side of me. I was a person full of rage and anger, a little boy who hated how he was treated when he was a child. But I never allowed that person to come out to harm anyone. I only used him in times of need, like during basketball or football. I also used him if I needed to protect myself from danger. But I realized some people saw that as an opportunity to use me so I could work for them.

They pursued me for personal reasons. I let my guard down because I wanted to show them the love I had inside of me. But that's when people misused me. Every opportunity they got, they tried poking the bear. They knew I was trying to stay on the right path. But more and more, they tried knocking me off course. Some of them knew my weakness. They were trying hard for me to fail, like setting me up with women so I could cheat on Jules.

They offered me things they knew I liked or tried quitting, like money and drugs. They tried their hardest to cause confusion in my life so they could get the best of me. The enemies tried their best to make me angry. Having a big heart often blinded me from the truth. I found myself falling for their traps. They strategized by using old stories about someone who I didn't like. They did this to get me mad so I could slip. Anger causes bad decisions. But God was with me, guiding me every time. On the flip side of things. I noticed things on Jules' side of the family. I watched them very closely. Her family started fighting and breaking up. This was at the same time President Trump caused major confusion and war. He was racist toward the Black and Hispanic community.

The world saw Black people getting killed on camera by White people and police officers. I lived in a predominantly White community, and I saw them act a certain type of way toward me. But to see Jules' family like this surprised me. Jules' family looked just like my family, but they had more money. People with money also have problems. They showed me their true colors, like manipulation and acting phony. I paid close attention to them because I'd never seen this side of them.

At one point, it got so ugly that it affected me and Jules' relationship. They had a big fight, and people picked sides. I watched Jules' dad pick his wife. I watched Jules' brothers pick their wives. So, when it came down to Jules and I, I asked a straightforward question: "When it comes down to our family, who are you picking?"

"You *and* my family."

In the heat of the moment, I watched Jules split me down the middle. That hurt my feelings a lot because we were about to start a small family of our own. Due to my upbringing, I needed somebody to be by my side and have my back, no matter what! A strong foundation starts with God. The spouses are a team. Strong couples are the ones who hold the house together.

I understood that Jules' family was her backbone. So, we both had a lot of growing to do. In the meantime, I continued to fight for education by telling my story to my followers and family members about my reading problems. One night, as I was studying, I got frustrated from practicing. My head was hurting, and I was tired. I laid my head on the desk and I took a quick nap. I had a dream, and an angel started talking to me. The angel spoke to me and said, "Dyslexia." When I woke up, I kept repeating the word, dyslexia.

I didn't know what it meant, so I did my research. I went right to YouTube. I researched anything that had to do with dyslexia.

I watched a few videos on teachers tutoring kids, but they weren't exactly talking about dyslexia. I saw a guy holding a book underneath a video called *The Dyslexic Advantage*. He was explaining what dyslexia meant. I immediately started watching his videos. He was persuasive and positive about dyslexia. First, I ordered the book. Then, I emailed him, thanking him for explaining what dyslexia meant on his YouTube channel. I told him who I was, and I was hoping that I could get more information about dyslexia. After a few weeks passed, I listened to the audio version of the book. I was freaking out listening to that book. It was amazing. It covered everything I was struggling with.

It sparked something in me. I felt like I'd missed so much in my life. I realized that I'm more blessed than I think. Jules thought that I was tripping out because I started screaming that I could see. I thanked God because He had opened another pathway in my life. Sometimes, you have to go backward in order for God to catapult you forward.

I no longer felt ashamed about the way I learned. I realized I wasn't the only one who struggled with reading. It was a whole community of people waiting to hear my story.

I also learned that what happens in the dark will come to the light. I couldn't control what other people did, but I did have control over my actions. This pandemic released something in the air. It wasn't just killing people. It caused people to be unbalanced. No matter what, I had to keep my promise. I looked forward to meeting my child and learning how to read.

Matthew 7:7-8 says, *"Ask and it will be given to you; seek and you will find; knock and the door will be opened to you. For everyone who asks receives; the one who seeks finds; and to the one who knocks, the door will be opened."*

Sharks in the Water

Once I started listening to the audiobook, I felt like I had a little more understanding of dyslexia. But I didn't have enough information yet to speak about it. I was so excited to let Jules know what I found. All my life, this has been something I've battled with. So, it felt like I found a cure to all my questions about my learning style. The next day, I checked my emails to see if this guy had responded to my message. Sure enough, he did. What I didn't know was I was getting ready to learn about the different types of "sharks in the water."

He told me a little about himself, and then we exchanged numbers. He did some research on me because he said he liked one of my videos on Facebook. We got to know each other over long talks. We talked for hours about how dyslexia affected our lives. I saw a few of his TED Talks about dyslexia, which were terrific.

He said, "If you want to be a motivational speaker, I can help with that."

I was in the middle of seeking a mentor. I followed the path God led me to. I read in the Bible that God will send you help while you're on your journey, so I thought this was good timing. This guy already had the experience. He knew a lot about dyslexia, and he was on the board of the IDA (International Dyslexia Association). One of my goals was to become a motivational speaker like Dr. Eric Thomas. He said, "I can help you with speaking engagements and also introduce you to some of my connections." He told me about a good friend of his who was famous. He was a motivational speaking training coach.

He said, "Normally, this would cost you. But I'll pay for it because we know each other." He offered me an ambassador position for dyslexia on his team. His business helped dyslexic people embrace their learning style. I asked him a few questions about his business.

"Do you have classes on the basic fundamentals of reading?"

"Yes, of course! That's the whole purpose of the business." He said he would need to do an evaluation on me to see if I actually had dyslexia.

I felt like I'd hit the jackpot. I was going to learn how to read, help spread God's message, and become a motivational speaker. This guy saw me as an investment. I knew I was the perfect person with my true story and background to become one the greatest motivational speakers in the world. I said to him, "So, let me understand something. All you want from me is to be an ambassador for your business and for you to be a part of my journey?"

He replied, "Yeah." He wanted me to look at him like an agent because I used to play football, and I understood that concept. He understood the struggles of being taken advantage of by other people. He understood how hard it was for people with dyslexia to get an opportunity in this world. So, over the weeks, we texted and talked to get comfortable with each other.

He told me about his family and his wife. I told him about my life story and how I found out about dyslexia. After I put that video up on Facebook, which was about me talking about my life story and how God helped me during my journey, many people reached out to me. Many motivational trainers, pastors, and teachers reached out. I thought it would've been cool to post on my page, basically letting people know that I already signed up with someone to help me pursue my dreams.

I felt like God blessed me because I survived all that trauma. I had just come out of depression. Little did I know, I was walking right into captivity. Before God truly blesses you, the enemy comes to test you. This man introduced me to other people on his team. He told me there were a few African Americans on his team, but I never met them. I only met white people. I met athletes, actors, lawyers, and a few business partners. This was exciting because these were successful people who all had dyslexia. Because we were in a pandemic, all of our meetings were on Zoom. I started the evaluation process and screening.

It was the weirdest thing ever because I didn't actually see or talk to any medical doctors. I talked to a few people over the phone. They asked me a bunch of questions about my reading, spelling, and visuals.

They asked me, "Have you ever worn glasses or contacts?"

I thought it was a little sketchy, but I didn't know too much about the evaluation process. When I asked this man if I needed to see a medical doctor, he told me it would cost a lot of money for the same results. Eventually, he said, "My friend, you are 100% dyslexic. Welcome to the team." This is why it's so important to listen to your intuition. This was a red flag, but I chose to ignore my gut feelings. I was so excited to learn about my gift that I forgot to pay attention. He told me about other greats in the world who struggled with dyslexia, such as Walt Disney and Einstein. He wanted me to start practicing my motivational speaking. He wanted to share my speech with board members. He also told me about his friend who was a motivational speaking coach. He said, "This coach is super excited to meet you."

He was pretty good. He starred in a few movies, and he also did a bunch of motivational talks in front of sports teams and other big audiences. I practiced early mornings and late nights. Of course, I took my Adderall to help me stay focused. I sent him videos, and he told me I was super gifted. He told me I would change the lives of people who struggle with this disability.

We didn't talk every day. But when we did, I always asked him about the reading classes and the dates I was going to start. He distracted me by talking about every other thing that didn't matter. That was another red flag! Every time we talked, it was about me meeting someone he knew who was famous. The people he told me about didn't make me excited. However, Jules and her family got excited for me. After a few weeks, I asked again about the classes so I could become a better reader. Once again, he avoided the question, and he only told me about the speaking engagements he had lined up for me.

I attended many video meetings. He was well-organized and detailed about everything. The people around him respected him greatly. But then, I encountered the biggest red flag. As we were in a meeting, I was about to say something, but he cut me off quickly.

"We all know how much Deon likes to talk, so we're going to wrap this meeting up."

Now, I'm not the smartest man in the world, but I do have experience with meetings and giving my ideas when it's time.

So, when he cut me off, it was more than rude. It was disrespectful and racist. All the white people in the meeting room got to talk. But as soon as I tried, he cut me off like he was hiding something. After the meeting, I asked him about it. Once again, he talked around the real problem. He didn't apologize to me. It was more of a, "Oh, I didn't know that I did that." Then, he started talking about an upcoming training with his friend. After all the recovery I did, I fell back into a deeper hole. I noticed I did everything this guy asked me to do. I made videos and advertisements for his business.

Every time we talked, he got even more manipulative about the things he needed. As I posted updates on my social media, he wanted me to stop sharing God's message. My story changed. Instead of thanking God for helping me find out about dyslexia, I thanked this guy for giving me an opportunity to tell my story. I didn't feel like myself anymore. As the weeks passed, I started overthinking. I didn't know if I was being used or if I was paranoid.

This was the worst feeling. In my heart, I wanted to do everything God asked me to do. I also had to trust in God's vision. I could see the start, but I couldn't see the end. As I went deeper into the business world, I realized I was going to need a life vest. Sharks are bullies, but they are not the only dominant species in the ocean. When you trust in God's plans, you learn His protection is all you need.

We are not here to please people. We are here to please God!

Spiritual Gifts

After Jules told me she was pregnant, we both decided we weren't going to tell anybody about the gender. We could let the world know about the pregnancy but not the gender. This was the longest, hardest secret I'd ever kept. It was exhausting keeping this a secret because I had to stay on guard from everyone who was trying to get me to spill the beans. I made a few people mad because their tricks didn't work. I didn't care. This was a promise I was willing to keep with God. Now, it was time to start my training with this guy who I watched on YouTube.

He trained in front of the University of Kentucky basketball team. He seemed like a neuroscientist because, somehow, he could get into people's minds and help them with their thoughts. To me, it seemed staged. But this guy had genuine talent. All our meetings happened on Zoom and were recorded. I was a bit nervous. The introduction was pretty long because we wanted to get to know each other. I'm glad I believe in the Bible because God talks a lot about staying on guard. These guys tried their best to get me to reveal the baby's gender. At first, it was unreal. They acted like they were my friends and tried to butter me up.

Then, I saw both of them doing hand signs to each other, like a baseball game. I didn't know what it meant, but I was wide awake and paying close attention. We reviewed the modules, which had four sections. We trained one time a week, and we touched on each of the four modules. In the first week, I was confused, almost hypnotized. Something didn't feel right. During my training, it felt like they were teaching me how to tell a white lie. Stretching the truth is what they called it. I couldn't understand because I wanted to walk in the *full truth*. I didn't want that Hollywood acting or the fake stuff. I wanted the real deal. I wanted to walk in the truth forever. After finishing that training, I honestly felt like he wasn't the right person to train me.

It was a good experience, but I needed someone I could relate to, someone who could keep it real with me and help me reach my fullest potential–mentally, physically, spiritually, and emotionally. After that training, I didn't feel like myself anymore. I felt like something was going on, but I couldn't figure it out. They both said I did an amazing job.

But I just couldn't get myself to be as comfortable around them. A few days later, as I was sleeping, my ears rang during the night.

Something woke me up out of my sleep. It was a loud ringing sound. This ringing sound was like a whistle in my ear, and it caused me to stay up all night. God was trying to tell me something. I needed to find out. We started meeting again as a team, and once again, this guy didn't allow me to talk during meetings. So, I paid close attention to everybody else. Something was off. I could feel it in my soul. I started working out again, running, and listening to the Bible. I prayed for answers.

That night, I had the craziest dream. It was about the guy who I was working with and how he was taking advantage of me. So, when I woke up the following day, I called my father-in-law. I told him I wanted to see if we could set up our own meeting together with this guy. My father-in-law is a businessman. I thought maybe he could use his professional judgment to help me see the truth. I wanted my father-in-law to ask him some tough questions as I paid attention to his body language. My grandma was always good at that. She made sure I was in good hands. Now, the meeting didn't go the way I pictured it.

My father-in-law and I had a game plan. During the meeting, this guy immediately took control and avoided everything we asked him. As this guy talked, I saw my father-in-law giving in on our original goal. It felt like they'd talked beforehand, but maybe that was my paranoia taking over. Either way, I took mental notes. He talked about how he had everything lined up for me and how I was going to miss a great opportunity. On one hand, I didn't want to blow my opportunity to make connections and follow my dreams. On the other hand, I felt like something was wrong.

No matter what, I needed to learn how to control my emotions. As all this happened, I learned how to use my five senses—or should I say six. God gives us access to the Holy Spirit, which is a spiritual gift. If I wanted to move forward, I needed to continue learning. Even though I felt like I was in captivity, it wasn't all bad. I got to see the truth in the world. I learned a lot more than I expected. I'm not chasing money or trying to become famous. I'm a real teacher with a real lesson. I'm learning that knowledge is power and health is wealth. If I wanted to swim with the sharks, I first needed to learn the sharks' patterns and the way they think.

Standing Strong through My Storm

Everybody faces adversity in one way or another. That's just the way life is set up. But if you're able to weather the storm, you're almost guaranteed to be successful in whatever you're pursuing. At this point, I still haven't taken any classes or gained any understanding of dyslexia. The only thing I learned was to embrace my superpower of Dyslexia. I couldn't understand how I could embrace something I knew nothing about. I knew I was gifted. I knew I was a blessing. But did this mean that I'd never be able to learn how to read higher than a fourth-grade level?

I felt like this guy was trying to cripple me. I had already done my research on the IDA Conference. When I told this guy I was about to sign up to join the conference, the first thing he said was, "I'm a part of the board that runs that conference." Then, he told me about the application. He explained that it was hard to fill it out. When I checked out the application, it was pretty lengthy. He talked me out of signing up by telling me that it was impossible to get in without his help. That was a lie.

He promised that he had all these speaking engagements ready for me. That's when I left my job. I was looking for a fresh start. This would've given me more time to practice speaking and traveling to other states and countries. Well, I did just that. I put my two weeks in and said, "Goodbye!" to everyone at my job. I figured if I told my truth about my struggle with school, that would help other young people pursue their dreams without self-doubt. I saw another red flag on a Zoom meeting. The meeting was to fill out the application for the conference.

Instead of me filling out my own application, he filled it out for me, which was weird. I'm more than capable of filling out my own application. There were two other members on the Zoom just to distract me. One of them happened to be a girl. During the meeting, she kept moving around, flashing her hair back and forth. This white man failed to realize that I'm from the hood. We are taught to stay focused when people play tricks. He didn't want me to fill out the application because he was mentally manipulating me and trying to have power over me.

He figured that if I could fill out my own application, I wouldn't need him anymore. On top of that, he knew this speaking conference was going to open up doors for me. He tried stamping his label on me just to show me off. This guy thought he had it all figured out. But that's the thing about lying. It's only a matter of time before the truth comes to light. In the meantime, I had a baby shower to attend. Due to the pandemic, I could only invite a few family members and friends to the baby shower. At least, I thought they were friends at the time.

I went around for years, forgiving my old friends, thinking they would change. But that day after the baby shower, I learned to let old friends from the past stay in the past. You truly have to watch out for the people you hang around. If you don't, you might catch yourself in a place where only God can help you. God sees everything, like the sun in the sky. Somebody, who I called my brother, tried to keep me from shining. He had a job to do, and he failed. That was the day I learned so much about my purpose. It wasn't my time to die. I thank God for saving me at that moment. You can slow me down, but you can't stop me. As the storm got worse, I stayed calm.

Everybody picks their own path. So, it wasn't any hard feelings after they failed their mission. Once the baby shower was over, I knew to wash my hands with them and continue on my journey. I asked this guy about the reading classes yet again because I remembered my goals and my mission. *I needed to learn how to read before my child entered into this world.* Once again, he came at me with idols and movie stars. I tried my best to keep my patience. In the meantime, the guy did have an event set up for me to attend. It was a baseball game with a few actors.

This was just a fundraiser to make money for his company and possibly make connections. The game was in a few weeks. He had people call me and ask me questions about my dyslexia diagnosis. I told them the truth about how I found out: An angel came to me in my dreams and told me about dyslexia. He didn't like my truth. He wanted me to tell people that he helped me find out. But I knew that wasn't the truth. He played mental games with me. He told me they didn't have tickets to the baseball game anymore and that I wasn't going to meet the movie stars. Honestly, I was cool with that.

Once he didn't get his way, he took things away from me as if he owned me. He only caused confusion in my life. On the other hand, I prayed that God could help me understand what I saw. My gut feeling told me that this guy was a fraud and a scammer. In the midst of the storm, I kept my faith. I never stopped believing. That storm came with dark days and low moments. That's why your faith has to be stronger than a mustard seed. When you seek, you shall find. Guess what God did for me? He blessed me with a baby girl on Father's Day! It is the best gift a man could ever ask for.

We named her Selena Marie Butler, and she was born on June 20, 2021. Selena came out with these big blue eyes and the most beautiful smile. I knew God heard my prayers. The day Selena was born was the day I became a king, a father, and a prophet. Christ Jesus was with me as I kept His promises. The King James Bible tells us that Jesus was tested in every way. Yet, He stood strong! I knew I needed to stand strong, as well. So when it was my time, I could help someone else during their journey. My family and Jules' family were so happy for us. Once I held Selena in my arms, that's when time slowed down for me.

Having Selena in my arms was one of the greatest moments of my life. Jules needed rest, and I was up like a lion protecting his family. I drove home, and it was the slowest drive ever. I usually drive fast. But that day, I was being extra safe and careful because I had Selena in the back seat. I had been through so much trauma. I overcame so many trials and tribulations. But after meeting Selena, it was all worth it.

I watched God be with me, even when I was going against things I couldn't see or things I had no control over. When times got hard, I didn't quit. I stepped right up, and I believed in God. I also believed in myself. That's when I received the greatest gift a father could ever ask for. I beat the storm, and now the storm is working for me! Prayer is powerful!

Enough is Enough!

I told this businessman and his team about God blessing me with Selena on Father's Day. I heard the fake happiness in his voice. I knew he wasn't really happy. He wanted me to believe in him more than God. What a fool! The following week, he had a few people lined up to interview me. The night before the interview, I fully confirmed that he was causing confusion in my life. Typically, he was detailed about things. However, over the months, he became vague when I asked questions.

It was just a matter of time before he exposed himself. Some people can dress up like sharks. But, deep down, they are catfish with tiny teeth. Being manipulative is a deceitful taste. Once you learn how to use that type of skill set, it becomes a part of your identity. I caught him using that skill repeatedly. Before, I didn't have enough evidence or knowledge to pinpoint what he was doing.

The next day, I did the interview. It was an Instagram live interview. It was about my life story. It wasn't a bad interview. I just knew this wasn't the right person for me and my future. My spirit told me something wasn't right.

The following week was the baseball game. This is where I put the pieces together. I had never seen this businessman in person. With eye contact and a handshake, you can learn a lot about a person. So, it didn't surprise me that he canceled at the last moment. He gave his tickets to a family that was in his dyslexia program.

At the event, I sat next to other members of his program, and they seemed pretty cool. I asked the family about the businessman's program, and the family's daughter told me her story. She couldn't read, and she was bullied as a child for not knowing how to read. She told me that once she started taking the dyslexia classes, she embraced her diagnosis. But she never mentioned anything about learning how to read *better*. Her mother interrupted every time we talked about the program.

It was so weird, but I did not want to waste all my time worrying about something I couldn't control. I wanted to enjoy my time with Jules and Selena. But it was hard trying to ignore the signs. I met people who owned the baseball stadium. This event was packed. But the fans weren't there to see me. They were there supporting the actors from the movie *That Thing You Do*. It was cool to meet them in person. They were down to earth. As the game went on, I talked to more people the businessman worked with. I wanted to get as much information about him as I could. As I talked to a few people, they asked me questions about my goals and beliefs. I told them that I believe in God, Jesus Christ.

They told me I should believe in Buddha and other religions due to the fact that I trained hard and ran a lot of miles. I also told them that I wanted to own my own business. These business owners started to tell me how hard it was to do paperwork and how overwhelming it could be. Instead of encouraging me to push through the hard part, they basically told me that I wasn't capable of taking on a successful business. I saw exactly what was going on.

They tried offering me money, but I didn't take it. I saw that other spirit in them. I put two and two together. As it got later in the day, Jules wanted to take Selena back home. I was good with that because we drove separately. After Jules left the game, I stayed on full guard. They invited me up into the owner box, where it was an all-you-can-eat buffet and drinks. This is where the actors and other famous people hung out. I was delighted to be invited. I didn't drink or eat. I was there just to ask questions and listen. When you want to become successful, you must ask the right questions and take notes. I wasn't looking for a handout, just keys to success.

Then, I noticed a bunch of girls eyeing me with their drinks. This felt like a set-up. These were the same girls who saw me with my family. The board member, who also was an actor, was excited because they had just raised $20,000. I had a one-on-one talk with him. He had been a part of the team the longest. After our entire conversation, it was basically either I was in or out. He kept it real.

I wanted to know how he was able to read his scripts for movies because he also had dyslexia. He told me, "Practice and repetition." I truly appreciated all his time. As more girls showed up at the owner's box, I decided to head home. They insisted that I stay a bit longer, but I wanted to get back home to my family. When I went back home, I did a lot of thinking. The next day, this guy wanted me to do a video saying, "Thank you" to the baseball organization for a great opportunity. I did! I had a great time, and I was thankful for the opportunity.

At this point, I didn't have a job, nor did I learn how to read. I didn't do any speaking engagements or get paid. I was being used like a puppet. This guy fed me breadcrumbs about being dyslexic. So, I took matters into my own hands. I set up a meeting with him. But this time, I was prepared. I knew he played mind games. So, I wrote a list of things I wanted to talk about so I could stay on topic. In the past, he always talked a lot. Those were just distraction techniques that would throw me off my game. I wasn't going to allow him to steal the show this time. Enough was enough. During the phone call, I watched his moves. I cut him off when I saw that he was using those old techniques.

When he avoided my questions, I made sure to stay on topic and redirect him back to the original question. He tried pushing my buttons. I learned that people can control you by using anger techniques. I told him calmly, "That isn't going to work anymore." I stayed level-headed and asked him the simplest questions. When you see a person getting nervous about the simplest things, you know they are hiding something. He used different levels of tone of voice, which is a technique of power and authority.

After seeing him use all his strategies, he knew I cornered him. I asked him, "Have you ever played chess?"

"Yes."

I said, "Checkmate." I told him, "God gave me a job to do. I know I'm gifted. I won't allow anybody to stop me from getting to the end goal."

He said, "Imposter syndrome." He said, "You're very good," and he hung up the phone. The next few hours, he sent out a coded message to the group email, then deleted me from everything. He took off running. I learned that you can take the easy way in life or you can take the hard way in life. Either way, there is a price to pay.

I have always been a diligent person. So, I didn't mind giving God the steering wheel so He could guide me down my true path and to my true calling. That's when God led me to the Eric Thomas program. Eric Thomas is a professional motivational speaker. Also, it led me to meet Mrs. Susan, who's now my tutor. It was like night and day. Eric Thomas helped me walk in my truth. Mrs. Susan taught me how to read. That's when she introduced me to the Orton Gillingham training, which changed my life. It's just a matter of time before the truth hits the surface. The business world is a big ocean. If you want to learn how to swim, you first need to learn what's in the water.

Always remember that everything that shines isn't a diamond. Every spirit is not from God. Patience is the key. Mastery is the lock.

Michigan Legislature & My Story

God gave me a direct order: "Tell your story to the world and go fight for education." After a few days of posting videos on my social media page, I crossed paths with a lady who has dyslexia. She told me her story. She also mentioned how her kids have dyslexia. What truly stood out to me was when she mentioned that there was a true way to learn how to read.

She called it the O.G. Method. At first, I thought O.G. stood for Original God, but it actually stands for Orton Gillingham. I didn't know how I felt about this lady because I had just experienced some of the craziest stuff with the last guy about dyslexia.

It was hard for me to trust this lady, or anybody else for that matter. But she was trying to help me. She saw something that I couldn't explain. My intuition agreed with her as she gave me pointers. This lady showed up with facts. As I learned more about Dyslexia, the businessman I used to work with started harassing me. He sent me emails and had other people from his team contact me to see what I knew. Some people just don't know how to take a loss. I finally felt like someone was on my side about this guy.

The new lady was extremely supportive. This lady turned out to be my college coach's sister. I trusted my college coach a lot. This made me feel more comfortable. The lady's name was Elyse. I talked to Elyse every day on the phone about Dyslexia. She mentioned how I could get evaluated the right way. Because I went to Central Michigan University, she knew some people who could guide me. Everything lined up the way I envisioned it. I picked up a job at Amazon. I thought it would be a great idea to go back to school since I had an unofficial diagnosis. When you work for Amazon, they pay for college classes.

I wanted to get my master's degree. I worked a graveyard shift, late nights, and early mornings. Every day, I went to work with a great attitude. I was positive. But I also noticed a lot of things happening at Amazon. I saw a lot of people sleepwalking, many of them just going through the motions. You could tell who was there for a paycheck and who was there as an entrepreneur. I also saw a lady going around stealing people's energy. She was always negative. She got people to complain about how hard this job was for little pay.

People actually fed into her negative trap. When she came my way, I shut that right down, and she walked away. Life is full of people with good energy and bad energy. When you wake up in the morning, you have a decision to make. I knew the mission and the goal. So, each day, I wanted to learn something new. I saw the way Amazon built its system. It was amazing. I compared it with a football system because it took the whole team to get the job done. I enjoyed working at Amazon, but I really couldn't wait to start school. I had to work at Amazon for three months before enrolling in their college courses.

Every day, I asked to sign up and get more information. But the staff was so busy that nobody could help me for a while. Elyse introduced me to Mrs. Susan. Mrs. Susan worked for more than thirty years in the literary movement. She also led the change with Senator Irwin in passing the literacy legislation law. Mrs. Susan knew a lot about being dyslexic, and she also was a tutor. After a few weeks of getting to know Mrs. Susan, I realized I was in good hands.

I wanted to tell my story to the world. But first, I needed structure and tools. So, I asked Mrs. Susan if she could tutor me and help me improve my reading. Not only did she agree, but she also allowed me to tell my story in front of Michigan legislators. At the time, they were fighting to pass the law for reading. For six straight years, this reading bill was denied. I couldn't understand why. This law was going to help fund schools and teachers with more training to incorporate the science of reading. This was going to be a game-changer. Teachers and educators would be fully trained and would be able to identify kids who struggle with reading sooner rather than later. This means all kids could have an equal opportunity to learn how to read. It felt good telling my story to the world. I was on live TV.

I spoke in front of big-time lawmakers. Many other people shared their stories and were fighting for the same cause as me. This wasn't just a Michigan problem. It is a problem all around the U.S. After the court hearing was over, I knew I had a lot of work to do. I realized why God wanted me to fight for education. This wasn't just about me. This was bigger than me. I felt blessed to be a part of a life-changing moment. The next step was to learn how to read. Mrs. Susan and I started training together like Rocky vs. Drago.

If you haven't seen the movie Rocky V, I highly recommend that you see it. After a few weeks of training, I was drained from work and studying. I finally got a hold of the administration from Amazon, and they told me they were only paying for employees who needed their bachelor's degrees.

I was looking to get my master's degree, so I saw no use in keeping the Amazon job. So, I made plans to put in my two-week notice. During my time at Amazon, I made a big impact on the people there. Every day, I brought good energy. I changed the moods of the people. The supervisor and admin staff saw the good work I did, and they offered me various positions and more money to stay. But I was only working there to go back to school.

After working the last two weeks, I finally called it quits at Amazon. This was going to give me more time to study and work with Mrs. Susan. During the first part of my training on how to read better, I thought it would be easy. In the middle of my training, I realized it's better to learn these things in elementary school and middle school. At the end of my training, I felt like I could be anything I wanted to be in the world. Reading made me feel like I could see for the first time without glasses.

If I can give any advice to any parents, teachers, or educational instructors, it would be to incorporate the Orton Gillingham method into their system or work with their kids at an early stage of life. Whether you struggle with reading or not, the Orton Gillingham method helps you become a better reader and writer. Throughout my life, I felt as if I had been lied to, cheated, and misled. I truly believe it was due to my reading struggles. I didn't have the confidence to speak up, mainly when I played football in college and the NFL. Now, I feel like I can own my own team. Many people say, "If you would've known better, you would've done better." I'm a true believer because now I'm doing so much better after learning how to read.

You can't stop God's plans!

Learning to Read

When a baby takes their first steps, they think they have full control until they fall down. That's how I felt when I learned how to read. The first session, I thought I knew it all. Mrs. Susan tried to teach me the basics, but I kept cutting her off by saying, "I already know this information." I tried to take control by just walking when I hadn't even mastered crawling. This means I needed to relearn the ABCs. I had to learn how many letters were in the alphabet and the sounds of each. Did you know that twenty-six letters in the alphabet make forty-four different sounds? I didn't know this at first.

I was twenty-nine years old at this point. I wasn't trying to hear about the alphabet. I wanted to know the keys to taking down the big words and applying them to my memory bank. This is why youth need to learn the basic science of reading at an early age. They shouldn't have to battle and fight when they get older. I was putting up a fight, even though I wasn't trying to. I fought with myself for half of my tutoring. I had to break my old habits. For me, this wasn't easy. This was going to take months, maybe years. But after all that I'd been through, this was going to be worth it. So, I was willing to learn, starting with the basics.

When I studied with my tutor, I noticed that I struggled with the smallest parts of the words. I struggled with the roots. Roots are word parts that carry meaning but can't stand alone. I was in my tutoring session for hours. Afterward, I was exhausted. My brain was hurting during the first month of studying. I was ready to quit. I remember saying to myself, "I would rather run fifteen miles instead of reading a book." But that's what I loved most about myself. I will *never* quit. I'm a trooper! When I start something, I must follow through with it. So, I went back the next month with a more positive attitude about learning. This time, I told myself I needed to become a better listener.

When I started listening, I started seeing the most progress. After tutoring, I studied by myself. Then, I'd read a book. If I wanted to become a better reader, I needed to have a sober mindset. As you know, I picked up smoking from all the stress. So, I had to quit. The brain is one of the most functional things that holds important information. So, I quit smoking, which was not easy. I went through some ugly stages during my quitting process. For a minute, I thought being high helped my reading. However, it only caused long-term damage. Every month was like a roller coaster ride for me.

Some days, I did well. Other days, I felt like I couldn't get out of bed. I knew this was going to be a challenge, but I needed consistency. That meant I needed to fight through the hard days by studying a little during those days when I lacked energy. I saw so much progress within myself. There was no way I was turning back. I felt myself moving forward and getting comfortable with my learning style. Learning the basics was the key. I needed to give myself credit for taking ownership and doing what it took to crack the code. Not too many people could stand up and tell the world they struggle with reading.

When Mrs. Susan and I were working together, she saw the smile on my face. She knew how hard I worked and how badly I wanted to learn how to read. To be able to smile in the midst of your storm is a sign of hope and prosperity. When my daughter started walking, she would fall down. Then, she would get right back up. That's how I felt. I struggled over a few words. Then, I would take a deep breath and break down the word the best way I could. Once I decoded a word, I would write it on a flash card and add it to my memory bank. One secret to becoming a better reader is to eliminate the distractions around you. During my time studying, I realized my brain was wired differently from other people's brains.

Not knowing how to read doesn't define if you're intelligent or not. I had no control over the way I was born. However, as I was growing up, people around me made me feel like I was stupid because of my reading problem. Then I realized stupid people don't graduate from high school or college. The dictionary defines stupid as "having or showing a great lack of intelligence or common sense." I laughed aloud because that makes me the opposite of stupid. I learned something new every day. I found out that Walt Disney, Leonardo Da Vinci, Albert Einstein, and Steve Jobs had dyslexia. They all found out about their dyslexia at a young age. These are some of the most famous intelligent people in the world. How is it that they were able to find out so early in their childhood about their learning difficulties? They had the right resources.

Their parents had the money to get them tested. Even if somebody had told me at a young age that I was dyslexic, I still wouldn't have been able to get tested because my parents didn't have the money. That made me think a little deeper. Why didn't my teachers catch my dyslexia during my time in elementary, middle school, or even high school? I'm not even going to get started with college.

Now, I'm thirty years old. For the longest, I felt like I was trapped in a box. This made me think about every child who is in this world and struggling to understand their gifts. What if we're able to train teachers and parents to help students unlock their true potential? Being able to read helped my brain imagine more. That's why Walt Disney was able to picture the unthinkable. He used his imagination. Now imagine Black kids growing up in poverty-stricken communities or on the streets and lacking the resources of education. The ones who can't read are the ones unable to use their imagination to the fullest extent.

These kids are being labeled stupid, bad, and ignorant. Where do you think they are going to go if they are not in school or working? If you guessed jail or prison, you are correct. The incarceration rates are unbelievably high when it comes down to African Americans in the prison system. It's 38.4 percent, to be exact! Unfortunately, 75 percent of them are reading at a fourth-grade level. I'm only speaking from the heart because I truly understand. I beat the odds when I felt like everything was stacked against me. If it wasn't for God, my family, and other supporters, I wouldn't have made it. I would have been part of that 38.4 percent statistics of people in prison who are reading at a fourth-grade level.

If there's a moment to make a change in the world, the time is now. Learning to crawl was fun, but learning how to walk felt even better. I'm healing and getting healthier. I'm embracing my future. I'm no longer looking at myself as a victim. I'm a champion. I know I enjoy walking, but I can't wait to start running.

The sky is the limit.

The Dyslexic King

When you do it once, it's considered luck. When you do it twice, people can't believe it. But when you do it repeatedly, it becomes a part of your life. That's how I felt about taking my education to another level. When I got my high school diploma, my family and friends were happy for me. But they still felt like it was luck. When I got my bachelor's degree, people said it was because I was a football player and I'd cheated my way through college. When I ran my first ten miles, people said it was the Adderall.

No matter what I did, people never gave me my true credit or respect. That's when I wanted to prove to people that I could take my life to another level. So, I trained harder. I read more books, studying day and night. I wanted to push past the ten miles. I wanted to run twenty miles. Not just once, but twice. Not just twice but repeatedly until people couldn't doubt my abilities.

I learned a lot from Eric Thomas, the number one motivational speaker in the world. He was teaching. I was listening. I felt in my spirit that I was next in line to shine above anybody who looked past me. I was tired of people calling me lucky. People needed to know that I'm a blessing from God. But, most importantly, my daughter needed to know who I am. I felt powerful after reading a book or studying. I could feel my confidence reaching another level. Reading and writing became a good addiction for me. I didn't want dyslexia to hold me back from accomplishing my dreams. I needed to reach my full potential without any excuse. If other people could do it, I could do it, too. I used to feel sick and dizzy after reading a book or writing a paper. But now, I feel mentally stronger.

I used to only listen to the Bible because I couldn't read it. Now, I read Bible verses and Scriptures. It felt good to hear myself read aloud. I found the wisdom I was seeking. The maze that my brain was in started being guided by the light. My dreams became a reality. After a few months of working hard, I noticed that I needed to be more organized and have more structure. I learned that this journey wasn't for the weak. It takes more than motivation to get past the rocky days. It took willpower.

I was battling this fight within myself. It felt good on my bad days not to blame others for my problems but to point the finger at myself. I didn't care what anybody else was doing. It wasn't stopping me from achieving my goals. My good deeds are my good deeds. The more you know, the more you can see.

From a Pawn to a King

10-10-24
Senate Bill No. 568

Sometimes, we wonder if God hears our prayers. Sometimes, we question God's orders and commandments. The whole point of believing is to build trust with God. At the beginning of my reading journey, I couldn't see where God was taking me, so I had to trust the process and have faith. Remember during the pandemic when I told you that God told me to tell my story to the world? God followed through with His promise. God was with me the entire time.

On October 10, 2024, the governor of Michigan, Gretchen Whitmer, announced that Bill 568 had been approved. I received a call from Senator Dayna Polehanki and Mrs. Susan Wardschmidt that the reading bill was approved. The governor wanted to meet me in person. Senator Jeff Irwin and chairman Matt Koleszar were also excited to meet me in person. They all have been working extremely hard to improve the literacy reading scores in Michigan. I'm so thankful for everyone who played a big part in helping pass the reading bill, especially the State Representative and House Speaker, Joe Tate, who was also a former professional football player. I'm thankful for the Michigan Department of Education and Elyse Presnell.

This was an exciting moment. I was being recognized all around the world—not for football—but for education. We'd just made history! The press conference was held at a middle school in Lansing called the Gardner International Magnet School. I celebrated with all the students because now they have a greater opportunity to build a brighter future. Once Governor Whitmer signed the bills, Senator Dayna Polehanki walked over to me and hugged me with tears in her eyes. Senator Polehanki gave me the first copy of the reading bill and said, "You deserve it!"

Yes! I'm crying tears of joy right now!

Trust the Journey

There is no magic potion in the world that can heal me from all the trauma I dealt with throughout life. But there are steps I took that caused me to overcome the pain and suffering. The first thing I needed to do was accept everything I went through as a child. As I got older, I realized that I was walking through old doors that I never closed. Once I faced my trauma, that's when I took back my power and ownership. I didn't fight with it. I allowed myself time to figure out the best method to heal from it. I thanked my trauma because it made me the man I am today.

Now, I am able to bring hope to others. It's true what they say: "What doesn't kill you makes you stronger." The second thing I did was acknowledge the things I witnessed and saw. This was going to be a challenge because the mind can play games, especially when you are seeking the truth in a tricky world. That's why I put everything in God's hands. If I ever get lost in the world, the Holy Spirit guides me back on track. Everybody has a mission and a purpose on earth.

Sometimes, we get distracted and lose sight of the original plan. Once you acknowledge who you are, that's when you find the truth. The third thing was recognition. When you are able to recognize the things going on around you, you will be able to take more control of your life. Everybody faces adversity in one way or another. It's a part of life. You can either run from it or learn from it. Always think twice before you decide. Your actions are what matter the most. When you recognize who you are, you will be able to see if someone is a negative person or a positive person.

The fourth step is nurture. After all I went through, I needed a hug. I needed to hug *myself* and forgive *myself.* I hated how my life started, but I love how my life is going. When I look back, it was a win/win. Once I started loving myself, I was able to love the people around me. You'll never know what a person is going through until you ask. That's why it's important to never judge a book by its cover. I hope people forgive me if I ever caused them any harm, and I humbly choose to forgive those people who caused me harm.

That's how I healed from my past. Amen!

About the Author

While many choose to wallow in self-pity after adversity, he's managed to use it as steppingstones to his great success. As a former NFL player, change agent and mentor, Deon L. Butler knows firsthand what it's like to build something great when everything around you seems hopeless. From poverty and childhood trauma to abuse, Deon was well out of high school and college before he realized his fourth grade reading level was holding him back. Later, being officially diagnosed with dyslexia, he courageously learned how to read at the age of 27 and now works diligently to empower children worldwide who may struggle with reading and writing.

What once was his problem turned into his passion as Deon helps people to embrace their gifts, embrace their learning ability and overcome adversity. After receiving a full-ride scholarship to Central Michigan University to play Division I college football, he managed to graduate from college and was later signed by the Detroit Lions. However, because he could not read and understand the NFL playbook, the Lions cut him from the team several times. Unfortunately, his talent on the field was not enough to hide his inability to read, so he was forced to forfeit his dream of playing in the NFL.

It was Deon's desire to read to his daughter that motivated him to pursue a personal tutor, who taught him how to read. In addition to winning the Unsung Hero Award and Bill Boyden Award in 2014 from Central Michigan University, Deon also received the Spirit of Special Olympics Michigan Award and was nominated for the 2014 Allstate American Football Coaches Association Good Works Team and Wuerffel Trophy. Recognizing his undiagnosed dyslexia, and a broken school system, allowed him to slip through the cracks, which ultimately cost him a permanent spot with the Detroit Lions. Deon works tirelessly to change state laws to prevent this from happening to other children. Through partnering with the State of Michigan and Governor Gretchen Whitmer, he was instrumental in helping the Michigan Senate Bill No. 568 get passed—allowing students of all ages to be screened for dyslexia early and get the literacy support they need along the way.

For more than five years, Deon has been fortunate to speak at numerous schools, government meetings, colleges and associations—putting him in the room with great men and women. From partnerships with Senator Jeff Irwin, Senator Dayna Polehanki and Michigan House Speaker Joe Tate to the Grand Traverse Dyslexia Association, BrainSpring and The Department of Education, Deon's work around the nation is having a ripple effect that cannot easily be erased.

In his debut book, *The Gift & Curse: One Man's Journey with Dyslexia*, Deon candidly shares both his struggles and triumphs through his journey with a learning disability. Not only does he offer quality resources for those who struggle with reading and writing, but he inspires readers to approach struggles with a sense of humor and embrace the strength that is developed from difficult life moments. As a beacon of hope and healing for many, Deon now defines dyslexia as a gift and finds great joy in helping others find strength within themselves to move forward with life despite the odds.